THE EFFECTIVE TEACHER SERIES

MOTIVATING THE DIFFICULT TO TEACH

DAVID GALLOWAY
COLIN ROGERS
DERRICK ARMSTRONG
ELIZABETH LEO
with CAROLYN JACKSON

LONGMAN
London and New York

Addison Wesley Longman Limited
Edinburgh Gate
Harlow, Essex CM20 2JE
England

and Associated Companies throughout the world

*Published in the United States of America
by Addison Wesley Longman Inc., New York*

First published 1998

ISBN 0 582 23155 8 Paper

British Library Cataloguing-in-Publication Data

A catalogue record for this book is
available from the British Library

Library of Congress Cataloging-in-Publication Data

A catalog entry for this title is available from the
Library of Congress

Set by 35 in 10/12 pt Times
Produced through Longman Malaysia, PP

CONTENTS

EDITOR'S PREFACE

This well established series was inspired by my book on the practice of teaching (*Effective Teaching: a Practical Guide to Improving your Teaching*, Longman, 1982), written for trainee teachers wishing to improve their teaching skills as well as for in-service teachers, especially those engaged in the supervision of trainees.

Although many of the books in this series have been written with a similar readership in mind, recent changes in the nature and pattern of education have led to the expansion of the series to include titles of importance to a wider readership such as head-teachers, parents, other educational professionals and those undertaking advanced study of education.

As specialists in their selected fields, the authors have been chosen for their ability to relate their subjects to the needs of the education profession as well as to stimulate discussion of contemporary educational issues among a wider audience.

The series aims to cover subjects ranging from the theory of education to the teaching of mathematics and from the assessment of special educational needs to teaching as communication. It looks at aspects of education as diverse as the teaching of secondary science and pupil welfare and counselling. Although some titles such as legal context of teaching and the teaching of history are specific to England and Wales, the majority of subjects such as teaching of statistical concepts and teaching as communication are international in scope.

Elizabeth Perrott

AUTHORS' PREFACE

Motivation is a topic of intense interest to teachers. At a time of increasing political concern about educational standards, and continuing competition between schools as a result of league tables, it is not surprising that many teachers ask themselves how they can motivate their pupils more effectively. For well over fifty years, motivation has been an equally intense source of interest to psychologists, generating a huge body of research. Yet most of this work remains relatively unknown to teachers. It has had remarkably little impact on their thinking, nor on their classroom practice. It is not hard to see the reasons. To start with there is little consensus on how to investigate motivation, let alone how to raise it. Moreover, much of the literature is written by psychologists for psychologists, and is quite simply inaccessible to most classroom teachers. In addition, teachers could reasonably claim that:

(a) too little research has been carried out for mainstream primary and secondary classes;

(b) too little attention has been paid, at least until the last twenty years, to the importance of motivation to *avoid* tasks set by the school;

(c) there has been too little emphasis on pupils who cause teachers most concern, namely those who are difficult to teach.

In writing this book we have sought to start filling these gaps. We have also sought to provide colleagues in schools with an accessible introduction to a complex and rapidly growing body of research. In Part 1 we provide an overview of the field and explain the background to our own work in primary and secondary schools in the North of England. In Part 2 we explain how this work has identified some of the complex influences on motivation. We show that although pupils with learning difficulties are more likely to display motivational problems than educationally more successful pupils, positive *and* 'maladaptive' forms of motivation are evident in *all* groups. More important, we show that curriculum subject can exert a potentially important influence, as can the school, the subject department and the individual teacher. Finally, in Part 3 we explore ways of influencing pupils' motivation.

Pupils respond to the same subject, and even the same teacher, in quite different ways. Responses to our work have differed almost as widely. Both from academic colleagues and from teachers we have received reactions ranging from very positive to very negative. We have not been surprised by these divergent views. Research into important aspects of school and classroom practice should not aim at a cosy consensus. It should aim to stimulate lively and constructive debate. That is our hope for this book.

AUTHORS' ACKNOWLEDGEMENTS

Much of the research described in this book was supported by Economic and Social Research Council Award No. R000232296 and University of Durham Special Research Project Grant No. 23019.

We wish particularly to acknowledge the help, patience and understanding of the necessarily anonymous teachers and pupils who took part in our projects. They were generous with their time before, during and after our fieldwork and we are most grateful for their support.

All names of LEAs, schools and teachers have been changed and identifying characteristics altered.

Note on authorship
This book was a collaborative effort. After the initial draft, each chapter was amended, and in several cases largely rewritten, in light of discussion and comments from the co-authors. For the record, though, the initial drafts of Chapters 1, 8 and 9 were written by David Galloway, of Chapters 2, 4 and 6 by Colin Rogers, of Chapter 3 by Elizabeth Leo and David Galloway, of Chapter 5 by David Galloway and Elizabeth Leo, and of Chapter 7 by Derrick Armstrong.

PUBLISHER'S ACKNOWLEDGEMENTS

We are indebted to The British Psychological Society for permission to reproduce our Tables 4.1 and 4.2 from D. Galloway, E.L. Leo, C. Rogers and D. Armstrong *Motivational styles in English and mathematics among children identified as having special educational needs.* British Journal of Educational Psychology (1995) 65, 477–87; and our Table 5.1 from D. Galloway, E.L. Leo, C. Rogers and D. Armstrong *Maladaptive motivational style: The role of domain-specific task demand in English and Mathematics.* British Journal of Educational Psychology (1996) 66, 197–207.

ABBREVIATIONS

A level	Advanced level of General Certificate in Education
CSE	Certificate in Secondary Education
DES	Department of Education and Science
DFE	Department for Education
DFEE	Department for Education and Employment
ESN	Educationally Sub-Normal
GCSE	General Certificate of Secondary Education
HMI	Her Majesty's Inspector of Schools
IQ	Intelligence quotient
LEA	Local Education Authority
NCC	National Curriculum Council
NFER	National Foundation for Educational Research
NVR	Non-verbal reasoning
O level	Ordinary level of General Certificate in Education
Ofsted	Office for Standards in Education
QR	Quantitative reasoning
SED	Scottish Education Department
VR	Verbal reasoning
SRA	Science Research Associates

Making sense of motivation

Motivating children who are difficult to teach: whose problem?

Introduction

At the North of England Education Conference in 1995 Sir Christopher Ball claimed that:

There are only three things of importance to successful learning; motivation, motivation and motivation . . . any fool can teach students who want to learn. (p. 5)

This commitment to the importance of motivation in education is illustrated in his regret that:

I often wish that we had spent as much time and energy and thought on the issue of motivation, as we have on the question of ability . . . The truth is we all demonstrate that we are brilliant learners before the age of five − because we want to learn to talk and understand. Whatever goes wrong later has much more to do with motivation than ability. For many people the key to faster learning turns out to lie in the strengthening of motivation. (p. 6)

Ball's conference paper identified explicitly two of the recurring themes of this book. First, by definition, motivation is seldom seen as a problem of pupils who want to learn. Second, the concept of ability has been less then helpful in understanding children's progress, or lack of progress at school. Yet his polemical approach prevented Ball from acknowledging three other equally important points about motivation.

First, every parent, teacher and child knows that some teachers are far more successful than others, irrespective of the children's initial motivation. It is pointless to debate whether or not Ball is correct in asserting that 'any fool can teach students who want to learn'. Some fools, and some teachers, are manifestly more successful than others. Second, and more important, whether a pupil wants to learn depends crucially on the teacher, and, as Ball rightly infers, the nebulous concept of ability may not be the deciding factor. Views of motivation which see it as something relatively fixed 'in' the child or young person are at best somewhat dated. Third, the unstated implication that pupils who 'do not want to learn' are unmotivated obscures the rather obvious point that some pupils are not just unmotivated; they are highly motivated to *avoid* engaging in educational tasks at school.

There is nothing surprising nor intrinsically alarming about the continuing concern with the motivation of a large minority of children and young people. It results from the legitimate concerns of parents, employers, politicians and teachers about the educational and social outcomes of schooling. If people did *not* question the attitudes and values which pupils learned at school, nor the adequacy of the skills, knowledge and qualifications with which they left, complacency and stagnation would be inevitable. Indeed, it was failure – or lack of motivation – to question the adequacy of the secondary school curriculum for at least 25 years after the Second World War which led to many young people in grammar and public schools spending as much time learning Latin as a modern foreign language, and more time on Latin than on any science subject.

Irrespective of whether they are teaching the highest achievers in the school, average groups or low achievers, teachers can usually identify pupils with high and low motivation. At a more general level, though, it is not the top 20–30 per cent of pupils who are most likely to be identified as having, or presenting, problems in motivation. Nor, interestingly, is it most likely to be the small minority of pupils with such severe and complex learning difficulties that their local education authority (LEA) has issued a Statement describing their special education needs and the resources for meeting their needs. Concern is much more likely to be expressed about the pupils to whom Sir Keith Joseph (1983), at the time Secretary of State for Education and Science, referred to as the 'bottom 40 per cent'.

For different reasons, government ministers and teachers are likely to agree that these pupils are the hardest to motivate to succeed at school. From the teachers' point of view, schools seldom boast about the achievements of these pupils. At the annual speech days, headteachers are much more likely to highlight the outstanding GCSE and A level successes. Specialising in the average and below average ability groups is not always the most obvious way to win promotion. For government ministers concern originates in the evidence that the UK compares quite well with competitor countries in the achievements of the top 20 per cent of pupils, but rather badly in those of the bottom 40 per cent. They are motivated by concern that the under-achievement of these pupils reduces the country's individual competitiveness.

The micro and macro political interest in pupils who could be thought of as difficult to teach illustrates two tensions to which we shall return later in the book. First, if teachers believe that their work is not valued, then *their* motivation to motivate their pupils will be reduced. In other words, there is likely to be an interactive relationship between the motivation of teachers and that of their pupils. That, however, presupposes that popular views of motivation as a facet of a person's personality are incorrect. If motivation is inextricably linked to personality, and if teachers can do relatively little to change a pupil's personality, then they cannot realistically hope to raise the pupil's motivation. On the other hand, if motivation is seen in social-cognitive terms, as children's responses to aspects of the situations in which they find themselves, the outlook for raising motivation improves. We return to these questions in Chapter 2.

Second, government aims of raising standards achieved by all pupils, particularly the lowest 40–50 per cent, cannot be seen in isolation from other aspects of education policy. The government which introduced the National Curriculum as a way of raising standards across the board is also committed to retaining the 'gold standard' of A level which is designed mainly for the top 20–30 per cent. Moreover, when the same government is offered evidence that its policies are succeeding, in the form of improved GCSE and A level results, it follows the tabloids into battle against the examination boards for allegedly lowering their standards. Such inconsistencies might be unimportant were it not for their motivational implications. It is not at first sight obvious how an intentionally exclusive examination system such as A level can realistically help to motivate young people whom it is explicitly designed to exclude. Nor is it immediately obvious why teachers' motivation should be enhanced by denigration of evidence that they have been succeeding in raising standards. In other words, motivation cannot be seen in isolation from wider debates about education policy.

Nevertheless, there are two reasons why this emphasis on the influence of national policy is potentially misleading. The first is concerned with the qualities and attributes that pupils bring to the school. The second is concerned with how these pupils respond in different settings. Pupil qualities and attributes which have been linked to motivation include personality, intelligence, gender and ethnic groups. It is not clear what part motivation plays in differences in attainment between groups of pupils. It would be odd, for example, to claim that differences in motivation level accounts for the high educational achievements of pupils with a measured intelligence of 120+ compared with those of below 100. On the other hand, there might be less difficulty in attributing the higher achievements of girls in virtually every curriculum area between the ages of 5–16 to higher motivation than boys to succeed on academic tasks. Moreover, it is possible that the effect of high intelligence is compounded by high motivation, and that the effect of relatively low intelligence is compounded by low motivation. If so, we would need to look at the educational policies, teaching methods and assessment techniques which might contribute to this effect.

Turning to how pupils respond in different settings, it is clear that they behave in different ways with different teachers. Moreover, these differences in behaviour extend to motivation. Repeatedly, Ofsted and HMI surveys have drawn attention to the variation *within* primary schools in children's progress (e.g. Ofsted, 1993). Similarly, a consistent finding in school effectiveness research in Britain is that differences between teachers within a school exceed the differences between schools (e.g. Reynolds, 1992). In other words, the teacher exerts a critical influence on the progress children make. In a secondary school, an instructive form of professional development is to 'shadow' a pupil or group of pupils for a day. They demonstrate unlimited flexibility in the ease with which they vary the amount and quality of their work, *and* their motivation to work at the tasks they are given, as they move from teacher to teacher. Rabinowitz (1981) described the process from a pupil's perspective:

they resemble large, and not very well organised, factories. In a factory of, say two thousand workers (pupils), a hundred charge-hands (teachers), twenty foremen (senior staff) and two or three Directors (Head and Deputies), it would be astonishing to find a work force that would accept a system in which each worker was engaged on seven or eight different pieces of work each day, for several different charge-hands in seven or eight different work-places, to seven or eight different standards. This, effectively, is what occurs in many secondary schools. (p. 83)

The implication of all this is that we need to recognise the potential influences on motivation. The range of these influences will depend on how we conceptualise motivation. Before turning to them, though, we need to consider what, and who, we are referring to when we talk of pupils being difficult to teach.

Who are the difficult to teach?

Galloway *et al.* (1982) defined disruptive behaviour as:

any behaviour which appears problematic, inappropriate and disturbing to teachers. (p. xv)

This definition is explicit in acknowledging that disruption does not lie 'in' a pupil, nor even in a particular act, but rather in how the pupil is perceived and the act is interpreted. The same applies to pupils being difficult to teach. One teacher may regard a child's learning difficulty or behaviour as the kind of challenge which makes teaching interesting and satisfying. To another teacher the same problem may be a source of endless anxiety and stress. Children are perceived as being difficult to teach when the teacher's sense of competence and control is threatened.

These concerns have a long history. In the last century the authorities had to call in the army to quell riots at some of the country's most famous public schools. At the other end of the social scale, Hurt (1988) has documented how the Poor Law was used to transport troublesome children to the colonies, a practice which continued until after the Second World War (Bean and Melville, 1989), except that the colonies were by then independent nations. Contemporary accounts earlier in this century show a preoccupation with children whom the authors found difficult to teach (e.g. Blishen, 1955; Lawrence and Tucker, 1988). The continuing debate about motivation, disruptive behaviour and learning difficulties may be seen as merely a more recent manifestation of the same concerns.

Conceptual models

Children who are difficult to teach create obvious problems for parents and for society as well as for schools. They can also be seen as problems *of* parents and society – and also of schools. How we think about them depends on our starting point. The term 'special educational needs' is needed largely because the pupils concerned are considered difficult to teach, at least without additional resources. Whether pupils who are not considered to have special educational needs may nevertheless also be deemed difficult to teach depends entirely on how widely we define special educational need. The Warnock Report (DES, 1978) recommended that policy be based on the assumption that up to 20 per cent of children would have some form of special educational need at some stage in their school career. Sir Keith Joseph's (1983) 'bottom 40 per cent' of pupils were exceeded in an influential inspectors' report which argued that as many as 50 per cent of pupils were experiencing some form of learning difficulties, and that schools should accept greater responsibility for them (Scottish Education Department, 1978). The problem is not, however, principally concerned with criteria for using a particular term such as special educational need, learning difficulties or 'disturbed' behaviour, but rather with understanding the assumptions implicit in any particular term. Elsewhere we have identified three areas of 'discourse' or debate in relation to children who could be seen as having special educational needs, yet only one uses the term 'special need' (Galloway *et al.*, 1994).

The 'special needs pupil' discourse The implication in Warnock's conclusion that up to 20 per cent of children may have special educational needs is simple. The committee was implying that teachers ought to be able to cope with around 80 per cent of pupils with no extra help, but could reasonably expect some extra support with the remaining 20 per cent. The argument was clearly predicated on the notion of help for the individual child. It was consistent with a liberal ideology of concern for the unfortunate and disadvantaged. Any definition of special educational needs would clearly have to include low- and/or under-achieving pupils, as well as pupils with emotional and/or behavioural difficulties. The implication of the 'special needs pupil' discourse is that the children, or their teachers, should be offered some special support, probably on an individual or small group basis. Clearly, in order to determine what form this special support should take, a careful assessment must be carried out of the individual's requirements.

The 'school and teacher effectiveness' discourse Research on school effectiveness has demonstrated the impact of schools on their pupils' progress and behaviour, arguing that differences between schools cannot be attributed merely to differences in the pupils' social and educational backgrounds (e.g. Rutter *et al.*, 1979; Mortimore *et al.*, 1988; Smith and Tomlinson, 1989). The educational implication is that problems of low achievement and difficult behaviour may have as much to do with curriculum delivery, pedagogy and school climate as with the pupils themselves. Research on teacher effectiveness, too, supports the view that the quality of learning experience is likely to play an important part in pupils' educational progress. A well-known study investigated the match in primary schools between the difficulties of the task and the pupil's ability (Bennett *et al.*, 1984), finding that many teachers tended to set tasks which were too difficult for their less able pupils and too easy for the more able. The focus, though, is on the teacher's work with the class, rather than with children selected for special help. There is little in the school and classroom effectiveness discourse to suggest that problems should be solved by giving pupils special work on an individual or small group basis.

The 'school failure' discourse This is essentially a political variant of the school and teacher effectiveness discourse. It is illustrated in political concern about the 'bottom 40 per cent', and sees the problem as a reflection of poor teaching and outdated ideology. (pp. 15–16)

Our argument is that the same problem can be seen in radically different ways. Each has implications for teachers, and each places pressures on them. The common element is the concern with children who present a problem for schools and/or who are seen as problem products of schools. The fact remains, though, that the assessment of these children has become a major industry, occupying much of the time of educational psychologists, teachers, school doctors and a whole army of other professionals (see Tomlinson, 1982; Galloway *et al.*, 1994).

Problems of definition

There is an obvious tautology in saying that children who are difficult to teach have special educational needs. If, as the Warnock Report (DES, 1978) suggested, children can be regarded as having special needs when teachers require help beyond what is normally available in the school in order to meet their needs, the same could be said of children regarded as difficult to teach. Tomlinson (1982) has documented a proliferation of labels attached to problem children, and has argued that these generally serve to legitimise the marginalisation of the children concerned from the mainstream school system. Saying that children are difficult to teach does not overcome the problem of negative labelling. It does, nevertheless, have the advantage, which the term special educational needs conspicuously lacks, of focusing attention on the problems these children create for the teacher. The evidence that teachers regard a substantial proportion of their pupils as difficult to teach is unequivocal.

Prevalence and implications of learning difficulties, under-achievement and behaviour problems

We have already noted the Warnock Report's conclusion that up to 20 per cent of children will have some form of special educational need at some stage in their school career. This conclusion was based on large-scale epidemiological and longitudinal studies of children's measured intelligence, educational attainments and behaviour (e.g. Rutter *et al.*, 1970; Fogelman, 1976). The research itself was meticulous, but the conclusion which Warnock's Committee drew from it was highly contentious and has been described elsewhere as a statistical artefact based on a political compromise (Galloway, 1985). It was a statistical artefact because the tests of intelligence and educational attainment were designed to conform to the 'normal distribution'. This statistical term implies that as many scores will fall above the mean as below, with roughly two-thirds lying within one standard deviation (in most tests 15 points) above or below the mean (e.g. of 100), and 95 per cent within two standard deviations. This enables researchers to select the proportion they choose for special study, or policy makers to select the proportion who should receive special resources. Warnock's Committee had no absolute criteria for selecting the figure of 20 per cent. It merely reflected recognition that a substantially lower figure, say five per cent, would have attracted criticism that they did not recognise the problems of ordinary class teachers, whereas a substantially higher one might have been ridiculed as unrealistic. In this sense, it was a political compromise. Its implication was that around 80 per cent of pupils should be able to cope with the mainstream curriculum without additional resources or support, but that a minority of roughly 20 per cent were likely to need some form of assistance. The conceptual model was that of the Special Needs Child Discourse, described earlier, with a firm focus on helping children with problems. In this sense the report was consistent with the benevolent humanitarian tradition of special education in Britain (Tomlinson, 1982).

In justifying their claims that around 40 per cent of pupils were under-achieving, or that around 50 per cent were experiencing learning difficulties due to an inadequately differentiated curriculum, Sir Keith Joseph (1983) and HMI in Scotland (SED, 1978) could have used exactly the same studies as the Warnock Committee. They would simply have used a different cut-off point. The implications, though, were entirely different. HMI's concern was to argue that schools should accept greater responsibility for the pupils concerned. While they did argue for additional resources, their principal concern was in reviewing school organisation and teaching methods with an emphasis on reducing the number of 'remedial' withdrawal groups in favour of more effective teaching within the ordinary class. Hence, HMI in Scotland was approaching special educational needs via the School and Teacher Effectiveness Discourse. Joseph, in contrast, along with each of his successors, had an entirely different concern. He did not believe that the alleged under-achievement of around 40 per cent of pupils was due primarily to learning difficulties and personal problems, but rather to problems in the curriculum, in the organisation and management of schools, and in classroom teaching methods. His approach to under-achievement was via the Failure of Schools Discourse, leading inexorably to radical legislative reform on the grounds that a stubborn profession had become incapable of motivating pupils, or itself, into achieving high standards.

Over- and under-achievement

Inherent in the Failure of Schools Discourse is the assumption that under-achievement is widespread, and that it can and should be reduced. Teachers, too, frequently refer to children they see as difficult to teach as under-achieving. The meaning of the term, though, is far from clear. At one level under-achievement is a vague value judgement, reminiscent of the old-fashioned school report: 'Could do better'. It suggests that change is possible, with an implicit distinction from low-achievers who are *not* under-achieving. Interestingly teachers never refer to pupils as over-achieving, presumably on the grounds that children who are achieving their 'full potential' cannot logically be described as over-achieving. There is, nevertheless, a clear assumption that with higher motivation and/or better teaching, under-achieving pupils could raise their performance.

The difficulty with the term under-achievement is that children must logically be under-achieving in relation to something, for example ability, the meaning of which is unclear. It is sometimes used as synonymous with achievement – 'a low ability class' – and sometimes as an assumed ceiling to achievement – 'working to the best of their ability'. The notion of under-achievement on a defined skill, for example reading, in relation to the level predicted by IQ has received considerable attention. The assumptions here are (a) that IQ represents a more global measure of an individual's ability than attainment in any single subject, and (b) that there is a positive association between IQ and reading attainment across the whole range of scores, even though this may not be so consistent within a more limited range of IQ scores.

Identifying under-achievement in terms of, for example, reading level predicted by IQ scores is likely to result in as many pupils being identified as over-achievers as under-achievers. It also results in a distinction being drawn between under-achieving pupils and those who have low reading attainments but are not under-achieving. The former group may contain some children with average or even above average reading scores, but above average or superior IQs (e.g. Rutter *et al.*, 1970; Yule, 1973). Children whose reading is retarded relative to their IQ have been described as having 'specific reading retardation', a term which many psychologists have preferred to dyslexia on the grounds of its greater precision and its explicit acknowledgement that other subjects, such as mathematics, are often not affected. Yule found that the retarded groups differed from the low-achieving groups in a number of ways; for example, the latter tended to have more neurological problems but a better prognosis for improvement in reading.

It is not clear how reliably teachers are able to distinguish children with specific reading retardation from those with low reading scores which are consistent with their ability as assessed by IQ. Nor does it seem likely that teachers are concerned principally with specific reading retardation or dyslexia when they refer to children as under-achieving. Whereas politicians use the term to mean that they think standards ought to be raised, teachers tend to use it in relation to an ill-defined concept of ability and psychologists to a prediction of achievement based on IQ scores. Yet irrespective of definition, surprisingly little is known about the motivational characteristics of under-achieving children. It is theoretically possible, for example, that low-achievers tend to make better progress, in spite of their lower IQ scores, because they are less likely to become discouraged by realisation that their reading ability is poor in relation to their other skills.

Behaviour problems

Repeated surveys have reported teachers expressing concern about the behaviour of a large minority of pupils (e.g. Rutter *et al.*, 1970). The surveys suffer from a similar weakness to those of learning difficulties. The questionnaires and check lists which teachers are asked to complete consist largely of items about which teachers are known to be concerned. If they did not, teachers would quite rightly regard them as a waste of time and refuse to complete them. Yet because they do contain familiar problems, the results inevitably lead to the conclusion that a substantial minority of pupils are identified as disturbed, maladjusted, disruptive or whatever label the researcher favours.

A consistent conclusion from numerous studies has been that boys are far more likely to be reported as presenting behaviour problems than girls. The same, incidentally, is true of learning difficulties, and there is a well-established association between backwardness in reading and behaviour problems, though this does not hold for reading retardation as defined above (Rutter *et al.*, 1970). Debate raged for years over the causal relationship: did anti-social behaviour result from backwardness in reading or vice versa? In their study of 50 London junior schools, Mortimore *et al.* (1988) found that with some children the anti-social behaviour preceded the reading backwardness, but with others the reverse applied.

It remains true, though, that most teachers believe that pupils who present behavioural problems are also poorly motivated to succeed in their work at school. Similarly, most teachers believe that learning difficulties are strongly associated with poor motivation. Yet the evidence for these beliefs remains tantalisingly elusive.

Educational reform and motivation

It is a truism to say that teachers can make any system devised by government, school governors or headteachers work effectively, or fail disastrously. One of the more consistent conclusions from research on school and teacher effectiveness is the overwhelming influence of the learning environment created by each teacher within her or his classroom. Yet the framework within which schools operate is determined by legislation. Since 1979 the education system in Britain has experienced more rapid and more far-reaching legislation than at any time since the 1944 Education Act. The legislation has been driven by a combination of economic and ideological imperatives, each of which have implications for teachers and for pupils, with particular relevance for pupils who could be called difficult to teach.

Economic imperatives

The 1944 Education Act maintained an elitist system of secondary education. For the next 40 years, some 30 per cent of young people were to leave secondary school with no formal qualifications. Until the beginning of the 1980s, almost all of them found jobs, mostly in the country's traditional heavy industries, such as engineering, mining and steel, which still required a large pool of unskilled or semi-skilled workers. It was of no immediate importance to industry, nor to the country's economy, that Britain was producing a higher proportion of unqualified school leavers than any of our competitor countries in Europe. Had we not done so, captains of industry and commerce would doubt-less have petitioned Downing Street with claims that over-qualified youngsters were refusing to accept the mind-numbingly boring jobs they needed to fill. Both schools and society had minimal expectations of those we might now consider difficult to teach.

Perhaps the most significant indication that this situation could not continue came in a Labour Prime Minister's speech at Ruskin College Oxford. Callaghan (1976) criticised schools for failing to respond quickly enough to the changing needs of industry, and launched a 'Great Debate' which led inexorably to the reforms of the Thatcher and Major years. These reforms, though, were only made possible by the largely uncon-scious alliance between the political left and the political right. While right-wing educationalists were castigating supposedly 'trendy' teach-ing methods in a series of Black Papers (e.g. Cox and Boyson, 1977), radical left-wing sociologists were producing a series of outstanding ethnographies which identified the failure of the school system to extend the life chances of a large minority of disaffected youngsters (e.g. Willis, 1977; Corrigan, 1979).

There was a broad consensus that all, or at least most, pupils needed to achieve the standards previously achieved by a relatively small minority. With the introduction of the national curriculum not only did all pupils have an explicit curriculum entitlement, but schools were required to ensure that the benefits were reflected in publicly available evidence such as examination results and the results of national testing programmes.

The motivational implications of these reforms for teachers are import-ant. The explicit pressure to improve standards did not sit comfortably with teachers' talk about 'low ability' pupils. The tension arose from deeply entrenched notions of ability. As long as the school system was expected to produce a highly educated elite, it was perfectly acceptable to dismiss a large minority as being of low ability and therefore, by implication, incapable of raising their achievement level. The more we talk of pupils as having low ability, the more easily we can use this low ability as an obvious and logical explanation for their low achievements. Most pupils are highly co-operative; if we expect them to have low achievements they duly oblige. True, they may find other ways to maintain their self-respect and their sense of belonging, but they seldom pursue the lost cause of success on terms defined by the school. The concept of ability and its implication for children's motivation is central to the work of some of the leading researchers into motivation, and it is one to which we shall return. Meanwhile, we need to note that economic imperatives interact with ideological ones.

Ideological imperatives

One of the more interesting paradoxes of the 1980s and 1990s was the drive to centralise control over the curriculum and education policy being combined with the increasing responsibilities given to locally appointed school governing bodies. Perhaps, though, it is not a paradox. Recruiting local cadres of party activists to implement policies dictated by the centre is a feature of governments on the hard left as well as on the hard right of the political spectrum. While by no means all members of school governing bodies are Conservative Party activists, it is certainly true that governing bodies have a legal duty to implement centrally defined policies. These policies include an explicit commitment to market forces, for example schools compete for children and get funded according to the number they recruit, and an implicit commitment to formal teaching methods and testing programmes within the school.

It is important to note that there was nothing selective about these policies; even though government ministers repeatedly claimed a preoccupation with the bottom 40 per cent, they also avowed their intention of raising standards across the board. Logically, attention should have been concentrated on the 40 per cent since it was these pupils who appeared on international comparisons to be under-achieving. The top 20–30 per cent had always done well. However, alongside the drive to raise standards of the bottom 40 per cent there was a deep ideological suspicion of the egalitarianism implicit in this. The only solution was to aim at raising *everyone's* achievement level.

The motivational implications were all too clear. The educational reforms combined public criticism of differences between schools with the maintenance of differences within them. While their absolute achievements might increase, the bottom 40 per cent would remain the bottom 40 per cent because an ideological mistrust of egalitarianism could never tolerate the 'flatter' distribution of achievement which would make it harder to identify the successes and failures both of the school system and of individual schools. If success is reinforcing to those who succeed, and if pupils whom teachers find difficult to teach seldom experience success, the prospects for motivating these pupils appear bleak. Nor are the prospects for motivating the teachers themselves much better as long as widely publicised league tables are based purely on high achievement, for example A level results and the percentage of pupils gaining at least five grades at C or above in GCSE. The next question, therefore, is whether schools can overcome the potentially demotivating effect of government policy.

Organisational influences on motivation

Primary and secondary schools in Britain have a number of organisational features which are not widely found elsewhere. To start with, primary schools have an organisational culture which distinguishes them from secondary schools far more sharply than the mere age of the children. In spite of official pressure to appoint specialist teachers, the overwhelming majority of teachers are still appointed as generalists, responsible for teaching the whole curriculum, or at least most of it, to their class. Moreover, even the largest primary schools with several classes in each age group are most unlikely to stream children by presumed ability. Children sit at tables and, in theory, the emphasis is on co-operation between children rather than on competition. In contrast, children in secondary schools are taught by subject specialist teachers, and classes are usually either 'setted' by ability for different subjects, or divided into two or three 'bands' of ability. Seating arrangements are more formal, and although the differences in teaching methods are less stark than is often supposed, there is a tendency towards greater formality. Children have to adjust to the change from primary to secondary school with minimal preparation. This could either motivate them to succeed in the new environment, or it could induce defensive strategies which serve to protect them from the fear of failure. In either case, the organisation of schooling has motivational implications.

These structural factors, though, may be less important than other aspects of curriculum and classroom organisation. Once again we return to the practice of ability grouping. At a theoretical level, the motivational impact of children comparing themselves with each other is controversial. It may be more damaging in secondary than in primary schools (see Chapter 2). The more important point here is that mixed ability teaching makes substantial demands on any teacher's organisational skills. Teachers not only have to monitor each child's performance across the curriculum, but also to prepare work which differentiates between different ability levels. In spite of evidence from international comparisons that the top 20–30 per cent of pupils are doing well, Ofsted inspectors are still quick to seek any evidence that the brightest children are being insufficiently 'stretched'. Faced with excessive demands, one motivational strategy is to give up; the task is avoided, or rather evaded, on the very plausible grounds that it is too difficult, and there is therefore no point in trying. This strategy can be seen in children, and also in teachers, when organisational or curricular demands become excessive.

A good example of excessive curricular demands came in the early days of the National Curriculum. The enthusiasm of each subject working group for its own subject led to a massive overload which made the National Curriculum in primary schools quite simply unteachable in its entirety. Eventual recognition of this led to the slimming down of the National Curriculum in Sir Ron Dearing's (1994) review. Faced with an impossible task, it would have been easy for teachers to resort to a course of least resistance, for example by concentrating on the curriculum areas of most immediate interest to parents and inspectors. For teachers, as for children, a challenging task needs to be realistic if it is to enhance motivation.

Classroom influences and the culture of teaching

At classroom level, each teacher's task is to motivate and interest as many as 35 individuals who never asked to be there in the first place. In addition there is a cultural norm that teaching should be more than mere transmission of facts; it should involve children in an interactive process with each other and with the teacher. This *is* a cultural norm. In other cultures, the teacher's task is more narrowly defined. In Japan, for example, the body of knowledge to be learned is explicit and discussion regarded as inappropriate. Rote learning and cramming of facts are standard practice, with extra classes at the weekend to prepare for the exams leading to places in prestigious universities (see Chiland and Young, 1990). The more open, interactive teaching processes in Britain may well reduce the body of knowledge that pupils acquire. On the other hand, it may create opportunities to learn different skills and to develop deeper understanding. For teachers it may create the possibility of greater job satisfaction, because the interaction with children is greater, but it undoubtedly also makes teaching more difficult.

An increasingly market-led and competitive climate may reasonably be expected to reduce the less successful children's motivation. If, as we have argued, these children are likely to be regarded as difficult to teach, and if teachers attribute their lack of progress to factors beyond the school's control, such as home background, personality or ability, teachers are likely to see little point in trying to raise the children's achievement level. The question is whether other influences can out-weigh the potentially negative motivational impact of unfavourable comparisons and of factors over which teachers have no control. There are good reasons for thinking that they may.

We have already noted the differences between schools and, within a school, between teachers on their effect on children's progress. Cur-rent ways of understanding motivation which we explore more fully in Chapter 2 emphasise the importance of people having a sense of con-trol over their environment. In their study of London secondary schools Rutter *et al.* (1979) showed that the more successful schools tried to involve pupils in decisions affecting them. Within the classroom, some teaching methods help to give children a sense of responsibility for their own learning, while others may have the reverse effect. Construct-ivist theory, for example, emphasises the importance of 'scaffolding' instruction. This occurs when teachers break down tasks into meaning-ful parts and

use modelling and coaching to teach strategies for thinking and problem solving, and gradually release responsibility to the learner. (Blumenfeld, 1992, p. 277)

If we contrast this with teacher-directed 'talk and chalk' it is clear that the two approaches make substantially different demands on pupils, and on teachers, but that constructivist theory encourages greater motiva-tional involvement by enabling pupils to make more sense of what they are doing. One of the themes we explored in our own research was whether different curriculum subjects encourage different motivational strategies (see Chapter 5).

Conclusions

This chapter has argued that although government ministers share the concern of teachers about the motivation of children and young people at school, government policy may be contributing to the problem. The same may be true both of the way we organise the school system, and of some widely used teaching methods in primary and secondary schools. Nevertheless, motivation remains an overworked and loosely used term. Too often, motivation is seen as a characteristic of pupils, perhaps not quite as unchangeable as age or eye colour, but neverthe-less firmly embedded in their make-up. We have argued that it can be seen as the product of an interaction between pupils and the vary-ing situations in which they find themselves at school. We should not assume, for example, that a child who is highly motivated to succeed in mathematics, will be similarly highly motivated to succeed in English. Moreover, motivation is too often seen only as a positive or as a neutral feature of pupils; they are regarded as well motivated or as unmotivated. We need to explore the possibility that some pupils may be highly motivated *not* to co-operate in classroom work.

Yet perhaps the most serious and pervasive concern about motivation is with the meaning of the word itself. Like related terms such as self-esteem or self-concept, it is used widely but loosely, and discussion is seldom supported by empirical evidence on how children in primary and secondary schools actually behave when faced with classroom tasks. Before moving to an account of our own research on the effects of age, gender, ethnic group, intelligence, educational achievement and curriculum subject on motivation, we must examine in greater detail how researchers in Britain and North America have investigated it.

CHAPTER TWO

Ways of understanding motivation

Introduction

Evaluation of children's successes and failures at school almost invariably includes reference to motivation. Sir Ron Dearing (1994) has recognised the importance of enhancing pupils' motivation within the national curriculum. School effectiveness research acknowledges the relevance of motivational factors such as self-concept, attitudes to school and to learning, behaviour and attendance as influences on school performance. Yet despite the political and educational consensus, the reality is that motivation is an elusive concept. The extent to which theoretical approaches to the study of motivation can help teachers to clarify the concept of motivation and use it in their professional practice is not altogether encouraging.

In Chapter 1 we argued that motivation is not independent of context: to understand children's motivation we must take account not only of their own personality but also of the social psychology of teaching and learning. The distinction has obvious importance for teachers. Teachers cannot reasonably expect to exert a profound influence on the personality of each of their pupils, but they clearly do have an influence on their progress and behaviour at classroom level. To see the extent of this influence we can draw on three sources of evidence. First, teachers know from their own professional experience that *the same children* make better progress and behave better with some teachers than with others. Second, this professional knowledge is confirmed by research on school effectiveness (e.g. Mortimore *et al.*, 1988). Third, Ofsted has repeatedly drawn attention to unacceptable variation within and between schools (e.g. Ofsted, 1993). Motivation is unlikely to be the only factor in these differences, but it would be odd to deny its potential importance.

This chapter traces the development of ways of understanding motivation from its early focus on personality to more recent work emphasising how pupils may respond to the classroom environment. We will discuss the relevance of concepts such as ability and under-achievement, and conclude by arguing that more attention is needed to contextual influences on motivation. The interaction between these, for example teacher and school subject, and between these and pupils' individual characteristics, for example cognitive ability and educational attainment, needs to be elucidated.

Changes in thinking about motivation

P. Marsh *et al.* (1978) have reported an intriguing study of a group of pupils who would be difficult to teach by anyone's standards. The subjects were a group of adolescent boys who saw themselves as having been written off by the educational system, and the aim of the research was to describe their perspectives on schooling and on football. Any casual observer of classrooms containing these pupils might instantly sympathise with the teachers who had done the writing off. The pupils were badly behaved in the extreme, constantly challenged the authority of the teacher and disrupted lessons on a regular basis and with a great intensity. This disorderly behaviour was also evident when the same young people attended their local football team's home matches on a Saturday, for here too they would appear to the outsider to be committed to establishing disorder and disruption.

The book reporting this research achieved some notoriety in its time due to the argument it put forward about the appropriate ways of dealing with the problem of football hooliganism which at the time was a matter of growing public, media and political concern. The authors' basic premise was that the apparent disorderly behaviour was indeed just that, apparent, and was actually based on a clear and well-structured definition of what was and what was not acceptable. Intervention by other authorities, for example the police, was unnecessary and indeed likely to be counter-productive. Leaving to one side the furore caused by this latter recommendation, the significant point to emerge from the research was that Marsh and his colleagues were arguing that the pupils' behaviour within the classroom was guided by what they referred to as the need to mark out a 'moral career' for themselves. The notion of 'moral career' is clearly a motivational one. The thesis advanced by Marsh and his colleagues was that pupils are looking to school, in its formal sense, to provide them with an opportunity to develop a moral career, an opportunity to make their mark, to be noticed. If they conclude that school is not, in fact, going to make this possible because a moral career within the formal school context requires academic success and that does not seem to be possible, then they turn to an informal school culture of their own making for the same ends. As indicated in Chapter 1, these difficult to teach pupils are not lacking in motivation: they may if anything be too well motivated and thereby unwilling meekly to accept failure in the school system in a resigned way.

A similar argument has also been developed by David Hargreaves (1967, 1982). He argued that anti-school and anti-authority behaviour act as a self-protective strategy to maintain pupils' self-esteem. Like adults, children and teenagers need to feel valued as contributing members of a social group; if the school and classroom do not meet this need they will look elsewhere.

Implicitly, Marsh and Hargreaves both see motivational problems at least partly as a product of the failure of teachers to meet pupils' need for recognition. This view threatens the self-concept of teachers as competent professionals. Moreover, it recognises motivation as a potentially negative force; it is not just that some pupils may lack motivation; they may be actively motivated against the school's goals. Before taking the argument any further, though, we must look at some of the earlier conceptions of motivation. These were perhaps less challenging to teachers, but also proposed a more limited role for them.

Drive theories

Most famously represented by Hull (1943), the notion of drive was developed from the concept of instinct and was seen as the source of energy for human behaviour. Hull distinguished between drive and learning. Whereas learning would explain the direction of children's behaviour, for example a mathematics or English task, drive would explain both the intensity and the duration of their behaviour, i.e. how long and how hard they concentrated on it. As drive was linked to basic needs, it would wax and wane as these needs were met to a greater or lesser extent. Hull also saw behaviour as being affected by habit, i.e. how accustomed children were to behaving in a particular way. Because drive and habit stood in a multiplicative relationship to each other (behaviour = drive × habit), it followed that a very low or zero drive level would ensure that no appropriate behaviour was carried out.

According to this theory, in as much as drive is equated with motivation, the pupil's progress is determined both by drive level and by the learning that takes place. The latter determines the direction and shape of the behaviour but the former the degree of energy that is exerted.

Such a mechanistic, or quantitative view of the nature of motivation does not preclude teachers from having a significant influence, but it is limited by the drive level brought into the learning situation by the pupils. The distinction between drive and learned responses is one that teachers often find attractive. According to the theory, their role is to encourage and facilitate learning by providing the right type of classroom learning experiences; the degree to which the pupils respond to these is likely to be determined by their drive level, or motivation. Drive has also been regarded as a 'pooled energy source' (Weiner, 1992) in that it is non-directive and does not necessarily lead to the channelling of behaviour in any particular direction. This energy source will be subject to variations over time, for example, a drive associated with hunger rises and falls in intensity with the passage of time since the last meal.

The teacher's role is then one of directing the available energies of the pupil. Teachers often talk of the need to channel a particular pupil's energies in appropriate directions or of having to re-establish an interest in an activity. These notions are close to the notions of drive and habit which were central to some of psychology's earliest contributions to an understanding of motivation. The prime point to make here is that the notion of drive serves to separate the notions of motivation and learning in a way that encourages teachers to regard learning as something which they might well be able to influence, but motivation, or drive, as something which is much more difficult for them to influence.

Differences between pupils are likely therefore to be understood primarily in terms of the *degree* to which they are motivated (the level of drive strength they currently possess) rather than the direction of that motivation. Motivation thus becomes a concept that can be readily used to divide the population of pupils into the relatively good and the relatively bad. Good pupils are those with strong drive levels who are therefore responsive to the teachers' efforts at teaching. The good teacher will be more effective at directing these energies in desired ways, but even the best teacher has no hope with the pupils who lack the basic motivating drive. These unmotivated pupils will be the difficult to teach. This drive-based conception of motivation perhaps helps us to understand why motivation often seems to be used to explain why some pupils are difficult to teach rather than why other pupils seem to be good learners. The presence of high drive levels provides the necessary, but not sufficient, conditions for learning to take place. Given a high drive level it is now up to the teacher to make the most of this. Learning problems for these pupils become a problem of ineffective teaching, classroom or school management. However, the presence of a lower drive level means that a necessary condition for successful learning has not been met. It is then likely that many teachers will see this as a problem that resides within the pupil, and one over which they themselves can have relatively little influence.

This does, however, raise a fundamental question about whether the assumed distinction between drive and learning is valid. An alternative conception sees motivation as an integral component of learning, with both being affected by the quality of teaching. Moreover, the development of other approaches will make clear that understanding motivation may be as important for high-achieving as for low-achieving pupils. These alternative conceptions enable us to see individual differences in motivation more in terms of how children adapt to a particular situation than in terms of their level of motivation. If this argument is valid, then the development of effective or adaptive motivation should be seen as an educational objective in its own right.

Behaviourism

Behaviourist theories offer one line of approach. The central tenet of behaviourism is that all motivation arises from basic drives, instincts or emotions in ways that are predictable. Therefore, teachers can plan what they wish children to learn and condition their learning accordingly; the question of whether children see the point in learning is irrelevant. From a behaviourist perspective, the amount of time children appear to be 'on task' indicates their level of motivation. An important implication here for teachers is that motivation is essentially an observable and quantifiable variable. Through appropriate reinforcement, teachers can increase children's motivation. Classroom interventions designed to increase 'on task' behaviour are readily accessible to teachers and presuppose teacher efficacy. However, Deci (1975) highlighted the potentially detrimental effects of external rewards and reinforcement upon children's interest in learning and continued (intrinsic) motivation to engage in classroom tasks. There is also evidence to suggest that competition for rewards promotes a surface approach to learning where children attempt to maximise their rewards at the expense of time and effort invested in learning (Condry and Chambers, 1978). That does not, however, imply that reward systems inevitably lead to a superficial approach to learning. Cameron and Pierce (1994) have documented circumstances in which they can have motivational benefits.

Another problem with this approach is that behaviour is *not* always predictable. Further, in its more naive forms it assumes that teachers condition children's learning, and overlooks the ways in which pupils and teachers interact in the classroom, with each influencing the other's behaviour. We need, therefore, to look at less deterministic approaches.

Towards qualitative conceptions of motivation

Achievement motivation

Probably the most influential advance on the early drive theories was Atkinson's (1964) concept of achievement motivation. Atkinson's theory retains a belief in basic tendencies which children bring with them to the classroom and which dispose, or rather predispose, them to respond in a certain way. These 'dispositional' elements are unlikely to be easily influenced by the actions of other people such as teachers. Atkinson did however introduce an important new element into his theory, namely that motivation can vary depending on how far success or failure are seen as relevant and important outcomes. In the classroom, success can be measured against a defined standard, and this provides a criterion for deciding whether or not that standard has been achieved. The standard can, of course, be set by pupils themselves or by teachers. This may affect the interpretation of success or failure but the basic definition of performance as successful or otherwise remains the same.

Any task requiring a pupil to achieve a certain standard can thus be seen to be double-headed. It offers both the prospects of success and the prospects of failure. Indeed, one cannot properly be considered to be present without the other. Any outcome obtained where failure literally was not possible could not be considered to be a success, and vice versa. Atkinson's theory recognised two different motivational strands each related to one of the two facets of achievement-related activity.

First, he considered the nature of a motive to succeed. He regarded this as a basic personality characteristic related to the degree to which individuals have a capacity to experience pride and other positive emotional reactions consequent upon success. Such feelings may also be aroused by the anticipation of a success experience. While everyone will experience some degree of pride following success, some will feel more than others. This extra capacity to experience such an emotion under appropriate circumstances leads to a greater degree of motivation to engage in activities which could provide a sense of achievement. It is important to note that this motivation is related to the intrinsic satisfaction consequent upon a success. It is not directly related to extrinsic sources of satisfaction, which may include the praise we receive from others, the approval of our peers, the increase in our pay packet or the gold star from the teacher. These all act as additional inducements.

Atkinson also recognised that people with the same disposition will not always respond in the same way to all instances of success. Some successes are more satisfying than others. (Again this is with reference to the intrinsic satisfaction that accompanies the success, not any extrinsic rewards that might be associated with it.) Similarly, the anticipation of some successes will be more likely than others to give rise to a positive desire to engage in the task. For Atkinson a key component in the determination of these differences between situations was the individual's perceptions of their chances of succeeding at the task. Atkinson expressed his theory as a series of algebraic formulae but essentially the perceived probability of succeeding has a direct effect on motivation and also has a further effect through influencing the value that would be attached to the success should it be obtained.

One of life's less kind tricks is to lead us to attach a greater value to those successes that we are less likely to obtain and a lesser value to those successes that we are most likely to obtain. The most readily obtainable successes are of course those on which pupils, and teachers, believe they have the highest chance of succeeding, and the least readily obtained are those they regard as the most difficult. On the one hand, then, we are most likely to find attractive a task where the probability of success is considered to be high. Such an easy task is attractive because it gives us the greatest probability of obtaining the successes that enable us to experience the good feelings that will follow success. Similarly we will be least attracted to those tasks where the chances of success are considered to be low. Difficult tasks can be unattractive because these naturally give us the lowest chance of gaining the good feelings that will follow success. However, a consideration of the value that would be attached to these different tasks complicates the situation. The easily obtained success offers a low value (essentially because it *is* easy to obtain) while the greatest value is attached to success in the hard tasks. There is a conflict, then, that has to be resolved. The resolution is obtained by looking for the point that gives us the most favourable combination of a decent chance of actually being successful and a decent value attached to the success should we get it. *Atkinson therefore predicts that the motive to success leads us to find tasks of an intermediate difficulty level most attractive.* These offer a reasonable chance of success, but as they are not too easy, they also offer a decent value. The success is still worth striving for.

However, this is only one of the conflicts with which we have to deal. The second major conflict arises from the motive to avoid failure which is itself associated with the prospect of failure. As stated above, any task which offers a genuine success opportunity must also, by definition, offer a prospect of failure. As Atkinson had argued for the existence of a basic dispositional force relating to the prospects of, and the experience of success, so he argued for a complementary dispositional force associated with failure. Pupils' motivation to avoid failure is essentially determined by the level of anxiety they experience as a result of failure. The greater the anxiety experienced as a result of failure, the less attractive any achievement-related situation will appear to be. The motive to avoid failure is so named because it is argued that the most effective way of reducing anxiety associated with failure is simply not to undertake achievement-related activities in the first place: *nothing ventured nothing lost.* A fuller account of Atkinson's work would demonstrate how pupils with a strong motive to avoid failure would generally be expected only to engage in achievement-related tasks where the extrinsic system of rewards and punishments provides a net inducement to start and remain engaged in an activity. Atkinson argues that individuals with a stronger motive to avoid failure than their motive to achieve success will be most attracted to tasks that are perceived to be either very easy or very difficult. The individual with the stronger motive to succeed, as noted above, is primarily attracted to tasks of intermediate difficulty level.

The easy and difficult tasks can be understood as being most attractive (or more accurately least unattractive) to the anxious pupil as they provide relatively safe havens. Anxieties can be reduced when confronted with a particularly easy task by the reassurance that failure (while it would be terrible if it did occur) is unlikely. The relatively difficult task also provides a haven of sorts in that while failure is clearly likely, the very difficult nature of the task provides a source of comfort. It cannot be so bad to fail at something that is clearly very difficult. We can see here that Atkinson is arguing that failures have their value too. Easy tasks carry a high negative value (failure under these circumstances is particularly damaging and anxiety provoking), while failures on hard tasks carry a low value (the sheer difficulty of the task itself provides some comfort).

This summary of Atkinson's work is perhaps sufficient to introduce some important notions that have guided our own thinking. First, and perhaps most importantly, it is suggested that individuals' first concern in achievement-related settings is not always with the prospect of gaining success. There are combinations of situations and people which produce an overriding concern with the need to avoid failure. This is an active motivating force in its own terms; it is not just the absence of a positive desire to be successful.

Second, dependent, as Atkinson sees it, on the relative strength of various basic motivational forces, people will be inclined to demonstrate either 'adaptive' or 'maladaptive' motivational patterns. The quotation marks around the terms adaptive and maladaptive need to be heavily emphasised. Adaptiveness is a relative concept. One's behaviour is adaptive in respect to some particular set of criteria. It is quite possible for behaviour to be judged as adaptive by one criterion but as maladaptive by another. Thus it is with motivation. Judged against the criterion of gaining success in the formal educational system, the predictions made for Atkinson's individual who is relatively high in the motive to achieve success are suggestive of an adaptive style. Being intrinsically most attracted to tasks of an intermediate level of difficulty is likely to lead to the maximising of learning over a period of time. Alternatively, the motivational pattern which makes these intermediate tasks the least attractive is likely to lead to patterns of behaviour that would be judged as maladaptive relative to the concerns of the educational system. A more detailed examination of some of the predictions derived from Atkinson's work further illustrates the compatibility of the two approaches. For example, Atkinson predicts that pupils with a relatively high motive to achieve are likely to want to move on to more difficult tasks following success and to backtrack to easier ones following failure. Pupils with the alternative motivational pattern, however, are predicted to display so-called atypical shifts under certain circumstances. This might, for example, involve moving to even more difficult tasks following a series of failures at tasks judged initially to be easy. Again the former pattern is likely to be widely regarded as more adapted to the needs and concerns of schooling.

However, adaptiveness can also be considered in terms of how it relates to criteria set by the individuals themselves rather than the school system. In this light, the actions and reactions of the pupil motivated to avoid failure can be interpreted as adaptive. If one's concern is to avoid the most personally damaging and anxiety-provoking aspects of failure then it is adaptive, under the right circumstances, to avoid tasks of intermediate difficulty level and to make atypical shifts after success and failure like the one described above. It is essential to remember that Atkinson is arguing that for such pupils the gaining of success, and the making of progress towards the gaining of success, is not the prime concern in achievement-related settings. If the most damaging consequences of failure, or the anxieties produced by the anticipation of failure, can be reduced or avoided altogether by taking action that perhaps severely reduces the chances of gaining success, then so be it. The risks involved in attempting success are simply perceived as too great to make the effort worthwhile.

The final point to note here is that Atkinson's predictions are not simply based upon the assumption that the motive to achieve success is low. Rather they are based on the assumption that these behaviour patterns are what follows when the need to avoid failure is high. Apparently maladaptive patterns of motivation are not just the result of a lack of motivation. Consequently, we should not assume that they will be found only in pupils perceived to lack motivation, nor that they will be dealt with by simply trying to increase motivation. It is the quality not simply the quantity of the motivational forces in operation that is important.

Before turning to the limitations of Atkinson's work we need to recognise that his approach was not the only one under development at this time. Richard De Charms (1968, 1976) developed a theoretical approach to motivation which also placed an emphasis on both cognition and the environment. De Charms starts with a nicely intuitive distinction between people acting as 'origins' or as 'pawns'. People acting as pawns feel themselves to be essentially under the control of external forces. They are pushed around by other people and it is those others who ultimately decide what happens, how it happens, and when it happens. When acting as an origin, however, individuals feel themselves to have control. One's actions originate from within oneself. In the following section of this chapter we shall see how these ideas have a number of similarities with the work of Weiner and the attribution theorists.

De Charms, however, is also concerned with the influence which different contexts may have on motivation. Some situations seem to induce pawn-like behaviour while others encourage a more origin-like response. De Charms is clear that it is better to act and feel as an origin rather than as a pawn. His school improvement work (De Charms, 1976) indicated that successful attempts to encourage origin-enhancing classrooms can have clear educational benefits for the pupils. This work also demonstrated that the effectiveness of his interventions was related to the extent to which he and his colleagues changed the context in which pupils worked and learned rather than seeking to influence directly the pupils themselves.

De Charms developed simple research instruments to assess the ways in which pupils perceive their classroom environments. We will be reporting our own use of versions of these in Chapter 6 of this book. De Charms would argue that if pupils move from an environment which they perceive to be pawn inducing to one which they perceive as origin inducing, motivation should improve. Our own interest in this related to the motivational consequences of transfer from primary to secondary school and of different curriculum subjects. For present purposes, this very brief reference to the work of De Charms serves to remind us that the classroom clearly can and does make a difference to the sense of control which pupils see themselves as having. As we turn now to the work of Weiner it is important to bear this simple point in mind as it is too easy to interpret much of Weiner's work as suggesting that it is the cognitive processes of the individual which count rather than the context in which they work. De Charms gives us an early hint that both individual cognitions and contextual forces need to be taken into account.

Weiner and the attributional approach

Atkinson's theoretical ideas have proved to be important. However, Bernard Weiner's (1986, 1992) useful surveys of the available work on motivation have drawn attention to the failure of evidence fully to support Atkinson's claims regarding task preferences (Weiner was, incidentally, a previous PhD student of Atkinson). While there is widespread support for the prediction that tasks of intermediate difficulty levels will be preferred by pupils who are high in the motive to achieve success, there has not been much support for the prediction that pupils who are high in the motive to avoid failure will express preferences for tasks of either a very easy or very difficult nature. However, it does seem to be clear that they have a lower preference for tasks of an intermediate level of difficulty. In explaining the pattern of findings produced by this body of research Weiner suggests that the information pupils obtain from learning situations are more important in determining their responses than the particular dynamics with which Atkinson was concerned.

Attribution theory holds that people *attribute* causes to events. It is concerned with analysing the ways in which people make decisions about the causes of events, and the ways in which those decisions might then affect a person's reactions to those events. It is possible to regard attribution theorists as presenting people as engaging in a relatively dispassionate analysis of the causes of events in much the same way as a scientist supposedly studies the phenomena in which he or she is interested (Kelley, 1972). A series of rules, or at least rules of thumb, are acquired as a part of the socialisation process and the application of these rules to particular sets of information will largely determine the attributions made, which in turn will help to determine the way in which the event in question is responded to.

The experiences of success and failure will help to clarify the nature of these concerns (see also Rogers, 1982). Consider two pupils who have each experienced a failure which appears to the outside observer to be equal. One pupil decides that her failure has been caused by a lack of effort, while the other attributes failure to a lack of ability. Weiner's analysis of attributions and motivation suggests that the first will be more optimistic about the possibility of success in the future. Both have seen the failure to reside within themselves, but one has attributed the failure to the 'stable' cause of ability and the other to the 'unstable' cause of effort. Differences in the degree of stability of the reason for an outcome are held to affect expectations for the future. Stable causes give rise to more expectations for the same or similar outcomes. Unstable causes lead to greater uncertainty in terms of what is thought likely to follow. It would follow, then, that a pupil who typically attributes failure to stable causes and success to unstable causes will have lower expectations for the future than one who typically attributes success to ability and failure to lack of effort. This would be true even if the actual pattern of success and failure were the same.

Weiner's analysis includes a role for emotion in the determination of patterns of motivation. Emotions are held to be determined by the outcome itself (we feel good if we succeed and bad if we fail) but the precise emotion experienced can also be influenced by the attributions made for the success or failure. Failures attributed to controllable causes are more likely to give rise to feelings of guilt than failures attributed to uncontrollable causes. Successes attributed to internal causes, i.e. something to do with us, are more likely to lead to feelings of pride than are those attributed to external causes.

The classic Weinerian position sees the perceived causes of success and failure being arranged along a network of dimensions (internal–external, stable–unstable, controllable–uncontrollable, global–specific, leading to intended–unintended consequences) with the implications of the success or failure being influenced by the location, on this network of dimensions, of the causes held to be responsible. Motivational differences are thus seen to be the result of differences in attributions. The attributions operate on behaviour via their effects on expectations and affect or emotion. In this way Weiner's work can be seen to be a continuation of the themes begun by Atkinson. Motivation represents the interaction between expectations and the value attached to those expected outcomes. However, in Weiner's case the expectations and the affect-laden values are seen as being a product of the attributional judgements that have been made earlier.

Thus Weiner moves thinking about the nature of motivation more clearly into the cognitive arena. The fundamentals of motivational differences are to do with the ways in which available information is noticed, interpreted and analysed. People with clearly different histories of success and failure might then be expected to demonstrate different motivational patterns (the more failure has been experienced in the past the more likely it is to be attributed to a stable cause and therefore the more it will be expected in the future). However, the relationship between personal history and motivation will not be a perfect one as attributions are also seen to be influenced by the individual's vested interests and their particular perspective.

In a sense, then, the personality component that was a clear factor in the theoretical system of Atkinson is replaced in Weiner's system by an information processing component. Expectations and emotions are still regarded as important but they are now seen as being only an indirect response to a particular stimulus. The mediating role of attributions is held to be of paramount importance.

Implications for teachers

Weiner's work raises interesting questions about classroom practice. The distinction between the task and the individual pupil's reaction to the task is clearly crucial. Thus, feedback which focuses on the difficulty of the task, ('Yes, it *was* hard,'), without suggesting a way of overcoming the difficulty would be likely to discourage effort in the future. Similarly, praising children for effort may simply strengthen their belief that effort is futile: even though I tried I *still* failed. Clearly, well-intended encouragement can backfire. That, however, raises important questions about teachers' attributions.

Galloway (1995) has summarised evidence that home background appears to exert relatively little influence on pupils' behaviour in school *provided evidence is collected by independent observers*. Evidence based on independent observations using time- or event-sampling methods consistently fails to show higher rates of disruptive behaviour in schools with high rates of social disadvantage in pupils' homes than in schools with low rates. In contrast, when the research relies on teachers' reports, high rates of disruption are more likely to be reported in schools with higher rates of social disadvantage. This evidence supports the view that teachers may attribute behavioural and, perhaps, learning difficulties, to the children's home background. To the extent that home background is felt to be beyond the control of both teacher and pupil, the potential consequences for teachers' attributions for pupil achievement are clear.

Yet there is another even more damaging attribution which teachers can offer for pupils' progress, or lack of progress. This is that they lack the ability to do better. If children believe they have failed on a task due to lack of ability their motivation to attempt the same task again is likely to be low. If teachers believe children have failed due to lack of ability, *their* motivation to encourage children to continue working on similar tasks is likely to be low.

Ability and learning

The attributional account of achievement motivation emphasises the importance of attributions for success and failure being made to causes that vary along a number of dimensions. One of the more important of these dimensions is held to be that of stability. According to Weiner (1979), stable causes, such as ability, give rise to a more confident expectation of more of the same than do unstable causes, like effort. Ability is frequently given as an example of a stable cause and most adult readers are generally happy to accept this. However, one of the contributions made by Nicholls (1989) has been to demonstrate that this view of the nature of ability is not one that is shared under all circumstances. Nicholls argues that young children are less likely to hold the view that ability is stable. For the young child ability, like effort, is held to be extendible. In other words, abilities can increase with practice and application (Nicholls, 1978; Nicholls and Miller, 1983).

Nicholls' work on the concept of ability led him to argue that pupils can hold three relatively independent orientations to achievements. First, they vary in the degree to which they are 'task oriented'. Task orientation is concerned with a focus on achievement itself; it is reflected in feeling pleased when learning and progress have taken place. Progress and learning are valued for their own sakes, and not for the advantages which they might offer in other respects. Some of these 'other respects' would be covered by Nicholls' notion of 'ego orientation'. The highly ego oriented are concerned with their standing in relation to other people. Doing better than others is what makes one feel good about school. Progress is measured by how far ahead of the pack one might be, rather than by how much of the task has been accomplished and mastered. Finally, Nicholls identifies 'work avoidance'. Here what makes people feel good about their experience in achievement-related settings is getting away with doing as little as possible. Work avoidance is the orientation of the skiver.

Nicholls' work complements that of Carol Dweck who has been one of the most influential of the North American motivational researchers. She has been concerned particularly with an attributional analysis of learning difficulties, to which we shall turn shortly, but in doing this she has helped to develop further an understanding of the nature of other fundamental motivational processes. Dweck (1985) identifies two fundamental sets of cognitions which, she argues, help to exert a strong influence on the motivational patterns which will be displayed in a variety of contexts. These are to do with beliefs about the nature of ability, and the goals with which a person is operating.

Ability, argues Dweck, can be conceptualised within either an incremental or an entity framework. Within the incremental framework ability can be extended or increased, while within the entity framework it is perceived as fixed. At the same time a person can operate in achievement-related settings with either a learning or a performance goal. As with the orientations derived from Nicholls, the essential difference here is between a focus on the task itself and the progress being made with it, and a focus on one's performance in relation to other people.

The important point made by Dweck, for our current purposes, is that if children hold an incremental view of ability then pupils with either high *or* low levels of confidence in their present level of ability can display positive forms of motivation to meet their learning goals. However, if an entity view of the nature of ability is held then it is likely that *only* those with high levels of confidence in their ability will be positively motivated. This leads us to the notion of motivational style and the work for which Dweck is best known.

The notion of motivational style

It should be clear by now that there is no consensus about the nature of motivation, nor even about the most appropriate way to analyse it. The notion of motivational style is even more contentious. Often, when we have lectured to groups of academic psychologists they have been preoccupied with it to the exclusion of any consideration of the results of our work. Ames (1987) has defined motivation as the systematic, qualitative response which people make to the various challenges and threats arising from situations in which either success or failure is possible. The problem for some psychologists seems to rest with the word 'style'. They have a legitimate point in preferring to talk about motivational *responses*. Yet if, within a particular context, responses are systematic, as opposed to arbitrary or random, the notion of style does not seem unreasonable. We start by identifying two motivational styles emerging from the attributional analysis presented above.

Learned helplessness

Learned helplessness is probably the best known maladaptive motivational style. It is maladaptive from the point of view of the school system in that it is likely to prevent pupils from making the most of whatever talents they possess. From an attributional perspective (Abramson *et al.*, 1978) learned helplessness arises from a strong propensity to attribute a lack of success to a lack of ability, and to see that lack of ability as being beyond personal control. Seligman's (1975) initial formulation of learned helplessness sought to demonstrate the wide range of situations to which the concept could be applied, and it is a concept that clearly seems meaningful to teachers. Learned helpless pupils will simply assume that they are unable to complete tasks successfully. If work becomes difficult, the learned helpless pupil will abandon rather than increase effort. Attempts to cajole them into applying themselves in order to achieve success are as likely to be effective as similar attempts to cajole the very depressed person into cheering up. (Seligman sees acute depression as often deriving from learned helplessness.) Attempts by teachers and others to offer help and assistance are likely to be interpreted as confirmation of the pupil's essential lack of competence. Once established, the learned helpless pattern is one that can be very difficult to break as the pupil has a view of the world which overly assimilates events into the learned helpless schema. Attempts at enhancing this view through deliberately seeking to change attributional patterns, rather than changing the pattern of success and failure itself, have met with some success (e.g. Andrews and Debus, 1978; Craske, 1988) indicating the appropriateness of regarding attributions as an important part of the process.

Mastery orientation

The concept of mastery orientation has been examined by several writers but most notably by Dweck (1986, 1991; Dweck and Leggett, 1988) whose ideas have been introduced above. All too often this positive and adaptive form of motivation is simply referred to as a yardstick against which other less favoured and less adaptive forms of motivation may be compared. As mastery orientation is in many senses the ideal goal for the teacher, this relative lack of explicit attention is unfortunate. However, mastery orientation can be understood as a motivational style characterised by a concern with achieving success, rather than with avoiding failure, by reasonable and realistic levels of self-esteem, and by a concern to achieve mastery over the subject matter rather than a concern with showing oneself to be better than others. This latter point is important, for it has implications about the ways in which a lack of success at any point in the learning process will be interpreted. Failure is not necessarily taken to imply a lack of ability that precludes future success. Instead, present failure is more likely to be regarded as a temporary setback which can almost be seen as presenting opportunities for developing more effective learning strategies. It will be appreciated that the mastery oriented ought to be more likely to display task orientation and incremental views concerning the nature of ability.

Limitations

While the concepts of learned helplessness and mastery orientation have a certain validity for teachers, they also have limitations. It is not clear that lack of motivation does always result from lack of belief in one's own ability as assumed in the concept of learned helplessness. In a most eye-catching title for a research paper Nicholls (1976, 'Effort is virtuous but it's better to have ability') neatly sums up the problem. Yet as Covington (1992) has gone on to argue, it may not be the success or failure *per se* which are critical, but their implications for the individual's sense of self-worth. Success can indicate the presence of ability; failure can indicate its absence. In Western culture, ability is a highly valued commodity and a sense of self-worth will be tightly bound up with the degree to which one can believe in one's own competence. Clearly, if one experiences a relatively high degree of success the preservation of a sense of self-worth will be easier than if one does not. However, as Covington (1992) discusses at some length, much of the success that is available in the formal educational context is competitively defined. As demonstrated in a variety of research programmes (Ames, 1987; Slavin, 1983; Johnson and Johnson, 1987; Rogers and Kutnick, 1990; Kutnick and Rogers, 1994) the effects of competition on the interpretation of success are powerful. Competition seems to have the effect of increasing the degree to which success is linked with ability. Competition also decreases sharply the number of people who can experience success. In the classic zero-sum game there is only one winner, everyone else loses. Covington (1992) argues that even those who would seem to be enjoying a relatively high level of success can experience high levels of anxiety because they are not being ultimately successful, i.e. they are not number one.

However, is it not the case that those who are currently number two try harder? The traditional view of competition as a motivator, which seems to underlie much of government educational policy throughout the 1980s and early 1990s in both the UK and the USA, suggests that this is believed to be the case. However, Covington's analysis of self-worth suggests that it will not always be so. At this point we can return again to a consideration of the role of attributions, but from a somewhat different perspective to that developed by Weiner.

Weiner's own research (1986) has demonstrated how people are able to make use of *causal schemata* in making judgements about the role played by different possible causes in bringing about a given event. Two people have enjoyed an equal degree of success at the same task. One has tried harder than the other. Who has the most ability? All other things being equal we would find it hard to resist coming to the conclusion that the person who tried less hard had the greater ability. Ability and effort are related to each other in predictable ways. The more effort exerted in order to bring about a given level of performance, the less ability is assumed to be present. The truly brilliant generally impress us by apparently achieving their outcomes without needing to break into a sweat! It is due to our understanding of these relationships (even though the understanding may be only implicit rather than explicit) that Covington concludes that effort can sometimes be dangerous. If we and others know that a higher degree of effort has been exerted, then our outcomes may reveal more of our ability levels than would otherwise be the case. If the outcome equals success, then the personal implications are likely to be acceptable. However, if the outcome equals failure then it becomes difficult to avoid reaching the conclusion that our ability must be limited. When threats to a sense of self-worth are experienced, therefore, we are less likely to feel comfortable about exerting the maximum effort. The notion of maladaptive behaviour once again comes to the fore.

Self-worth motivation

As was argued above, however, in relation to the work of Atkinson, the notion of maladaptiveness has to be understood relative to the individuals' goals. If the goal is concerned with maximising performance and learning, then any feeling that the exertion of effort might be personally dangerous is clearly maladaptive. While Covington would recognise the Yerkes-Dobson law (which states that too much arousal, as well as too little may undermine performance) most teachers would argue that insufficient effort was a greater problem with the difficult to teach than too much. However, Covington is able to demonstrate that insufficient effort can itself be a consequence of too much arousal.

High arousal, or anxiety, inhibits performance in at least two ways. First, the anxiety itself can prevent pupils from demonstrating what they have, in fact, already learnt. However, anxiety can also bring into play self-defensive mechanisms where the reduction of effort, and possibly therefore the diminution of performance, is strategic. It is this strategic use of defensive mechanisms (which may include the reduction of effort, but also procrastination, aiming too high, aiming too low and cheating (Covington, 1992)) that is the essence of the self-worth motive. Behaviours which are maladaptive in respect to improving performance may be highly adaptive in respect to maintaining the best possible sense of self-worth when failure threatens. It is what one is aiming to do that counts.

In common with learned helplessness, the individual's confidence in their own level of ability lies at the heart of the self-worth motive. However, whereas learned helpless pupils have effectively abandoned hope as far as their ability level is concerned, individuals governed by the self-worth motive still have the belief that they have, or may have, the necessary degree of competence, but are not certain. This does, however, indicate a limitation in Covington's theory. It is based on the twin premises: (a) that academic success is a culturally valued commodity; (b) that pupils protect their self-esteem from possible failure to achieve academic success. These premises may not always be valid. For example, some pupils may reject the goal of academic success in order to maintain their status in their peer group, not because they fear academic failure. This argument has obvious links with the work of P. Marsh *et al.* (1978) and Hargreaves (1982) mentioned earlier in the chapter. Nevertheless,

Covington's work has shown how defensive strategies may often be seen as necessary in order to protect self-esteem against the possible or anticipated effects of failure. We have also seen how these self-defensive strategies, including procrastination and devaluation of the task will often be maladaptive from the point of view of enhancing progress. Individuals who demonstrate the self-worth motivated style are simply those who most clearly demonstrate this particular pattern of behaviour and concerns.

Conclusions

This chapter has provided a brief review of the work of the principle motivation theorists, such as Atkinson, Weiner, Nicholls, Dweck and Covington. We have noted Nicholls' distinction between task orientation, ego involvement and work avoidance and have identified three motivational styles based largely on the work of Dweck and Covington: mastery orientation, learned helplessness and self-worth motivation. While these should not be seen as all-inclusive, the contrast between adaptive and maladaptive motivational styles, and also between two maladaptive styles, offers a useful framework for further investigation of motivation in relation to pupils who are difficult to teach. Before any further investigation is possible, though, we need to show that each of the broad types of theory with which the researchers have been associated carries with it a different set of assumptions about the nature of motivation.

Ames' (1987) definition (see p. 33) implies that motivational style is a recognisable and consistent pattern of responses to particular contexts. However, Ames' definition does not make it clear whether consistency is a function of the individual who is displaying the style, or of the context within which the display takes place. In other words style can be considered to be a property of the pupil, something which he or she brings into the situation and which determines the way in which they respond. The style would belong to the person and would be expected therefore to show some degree of consistency over different times and contexts. Alternatively, motivational style, although of course displayed by individual people, can be regarded as a prime function of the context. Some situations will be likely to produce a greater display of one style than others almost irrespective of the nature of the individuals within them.

Thirdly, both of the above may be possible and style is best understood as the outcome of interactions between individuals and contexts in which both play a part but in which neither on its own determines the styles displayed. Let us then briefly consider how the various broad theoretical positions discussed above might have a bearing on the nature of motivational style.

Possible bases for beliefs concerning the determinants of motivational style

1. Personality

The theoretical approach to achievement motivation provided by Atkinson and Raynol (1974, 1978) offers one starting point. As we have seen, Atkinson's position is one that gives a prominent role to the nature of relatively stable and deep-rooted personality traits. The adoption of the view that motivational style stems from differences in such personality traits would encourage the view that motivational style is established relatively early in life and is brought into the classroom with the child. There would be little that the classroom teacher could do to effect change. Such a conception would therefore imply relatively low levels of teacher efficacy with regard to developing more adaptive forms of motivation than those already found in the classroom. The child's home background and significant early experiences would be judged to be more important determinants of motivational style than would current school-based experiences. It should also follow that such a conception would lead to the view that a child would show similar motivational patterns across a range of situations, both within school and between school and non-school settings.

2. Information processing

Strongly associated with the attributional approach of Weiner is the view that motivational style reflects the culmination of the child's exposure to given patterns of information. When conceived in information processing terms, the attributional approach to motivation suggests that individuals will each apply essentially the same sets of rules (these being perhaps culturally determined) to varying sets of information. Persistent failure in an area of work will give rise to different attributions from those produced by intermittent or very occasional failure. Motivational style develops as the pattern of information, for example about success or failure, becomes more clearly established and begins to interact with the attributional process in order to produce a consistent and repeated response to given situations.

Such a conception suggests that changes to the pattern of information may succeed in producing changes to the underlying motivational style, but that one would have to attend to the attributional responses as well. For example, changing a teaching method to enable pupils to achieve success more frequently *may* produce a change in motivational style, but this will not necessarily be the case if they attribute their success to luck or to the task having been made too easy. However, it can be noted that the degree to which effective change is judged to be possible will depend largely on the extent to which the informational and attributional patterns have become entrenched. Thus, the more a teacher believes that a well-established pattern has been created, the less she/he is likely to accept that effective remedial action is possible. Secondary school teachers might therefore produce less optimistic prognoses in terms of the changes that might be possible than will primary school teachers. This in turn might help to produce greater stability in the motivational styles of older children in addition to the effects of an accumulating history of given levels of success and failure.

3. Goals and related cognitions

The final example of a basis for motivational style can be taken from the work of Dweck, Nicholls and Covington examining the various cognitions associated with the styles of learned helplessness, self-worth motivation and mastery orientation. These authors are each essentially arguing that the pattern of motivation displayed by an individual is a function of the beliefs and goals that a person adheres to *at that time*. The emphasis is important, for it is quite possible under this conception that the style of an individual will be subject to change as they move from one context to another. The work of H.W. Marsh and his colleagues (1988) in connection with the self-concept in educational contexts is increasingly making it clear that self-directed beliefs are variable across different parts of the education system. Specifically Marsh has argued that self-concepts in English need not have a simple and direct relationship to those held in mathematics. So it may well be with the self-beliefs and goals associated with motivational style. A set of beliefs that apply in one subject, or even more likely in one school or with one teacher, need not apply when the context changes. Such a view offers the prospect of concluding that motivational styles can indeed be influenced by the behaviour of teachers and offers a useful additional perspective on the debate concerning effective schools and effective teachers.

In essence, then, motivational style need not be characterised simply as a property of the individual pupil. Style *may* be a function of personality and may therefore, once established, become stable across different contexts. Style *may* be a function of the context itself, so while that context typically produces, say, a mastery oriented response, those same people will not necessarily carry that positive style with them into other, less favourable, contexts. Style *may* be the result of interactions between personal and situational influences. Individuals bring with them orientations which might dispose them towards one style or another, but those orientations are subject to the influence of the relevant parameters of the situation in such a way as to make the prediction of style on the basis of information concerning the individual alone a hazardous process. In the next chapter we look at ways of investigating these questions.

CHAPTER THREE

Teaching and motivational style

Introduction

It would not be unreasonable to conclude from Chapter 2 that researchers have not discovered a great deal of immediate practical value for teachers' classroom practice. They do not agree on the nature of motivation, for example whether it should be seen as a function of personality, context, or an interaction between the two, and as a result there is little consensus on how to investigate it. Perhaps, though, we should not be too disheartened.

A school system in which all pupils were highly motivated to succeed on teacher-directed tasks would be one in which all pupils acquiesced in everything their teachers required. Similarly a classroom in which the teacher only gave directions which were in tune with the pupils' motivations would be one in which the teacher might find it impossible to insist on work which lacked intrinsic motivational attraction. Some necessary work will always lack intrinsic appeal. Fortunately neither situation is ever likely to arise. Conflict is inherent in education for at least three reasons. First, teaching requires one person to define a task and motivate a lot of other people to work at it. Not surprisingly, the other people vary in their commitment to the tasks set. Second, schools, like all other social groups, require rules and the existence of rules necessarily implies the possibility of breaking them. Third, given the competitive nature of Western society it follows that some pupils, and some schools, will be less successful than others. Yet the least successful pupils are seen as problems, and are likely to see themselves as such . . . Hence, it is not possible to envisage a school system in which all pupils are easy to motivate and no pupils are seen as difficult to teach.

The motivation of difficult to teach pupils, though, is likely to vary as widely as their behaviour and their educational progress. A few will be driven by the possibility of success. Interestingly, this assumption lies behind the rhetoric not only of government ministers but also of many teachers. Others may be more influenced by the fear of failure. Of these, some will genuinely believe that they lack the skills or ability to compete successfully. Others may find plausible reasons for not competing: 'I *could* get a good mark in my course work but I think it's more important to show my commitment to the school/university rugby team', or just 'to mess around with my mates and enjoy myself'.

The point is that no unidimensional theory of motivation is convincing. If motivation were a straightforward concept it would be uninteresting. The challenge is to find ways of conceptualising it which help teachers to understand children's progress and behaviour, thereby helping them to evaluate their classroom practice and teaching methods.

The first part of this chapter asks whether concepts of motivation derived from the theoretical literature are meaningful to teachers and distinguish between children who are difficult to teach and other children. We shall argue that the evidence is generally positive, but suggests that theories which see motivation mainly as a function of personality should be treated with caution. The second part of the chapter will consider what information teachers might find useful about pupils' motivational styles in different classroom settings. This question, of course, focuses attention not only on possible differences between groups of pupils, for example those with differing levels of educational attainment, but also on aspects of the curriculum.

Teachers' assessments of motivational style

Some research questions

In educational discourse, strength of belief in something often seems to be inversely related to evidence for the belief: the less evidence, the stronger the belief, or 'don't confuse me with evidence; I know it's true.' The belief that pupils who are difficult to teach lack motivation to learn has become part of the conventional wisdom in many staffrooms, and we have argued that these pupils have special educational needs as defined in the Warnock Report (DES, 1978) and subsequent legislation. Yet there is a remarkable dearth of empirical evidence about the relationships between motivational style and learning or behavioural difficulties. Nor is there much evidence on whether theoretically derived conceptions of motivation are meaningful to teachers. Only if we can show that there *is* a relationship between learning and/or behavioural difficulties and motivational style as assessed by teachers will there be a sound basis for exploring pupils' motivational styles in the classroom.

In one of our first studies we set out to answer five questions (see Leo and Galloway, 1994):

- Do primary school teachers understand motivational style in terms of children's classroom behaviour generally, or are there significant differences in their perceptions of children's motivational style and behaviour across subjects such as English and mathematics?

- Are the theoretically-driven motivational styles of mastery orientation, learned helplessness and self-worth motivation relevant and meaningful to primary school teachers in a classroom context?
- Which of the above motivational styles, if any, do primary school teachers associate with children experiencing learning and/or behavioural difficulties? Are these motivational styles associated more with particular types of learning or behavioural difficulties?
- Are there significant differences in the number of girls and boys that primary school teachers identify within each of the three motivational styles?
- Are there significant differences between teachers in the number of children they identify within each motivational style?

To answer these questions we designed a nine-item questionnaire. The first four items asked teachers of five Year 6 primary classes (ages 10–11) to rate each pupil on four possible indications of special educational need: low ability, under-achieving, socially isolated and trouble-some behaviour. In each case a short descriptive explanation was given, for example for low ability: 'Is significantly behind other pupils in the year group but is probably not under-achieving in relation to her/his ability.' The next three items investigated aspects of motivation derived from research described in Chapter 2: learned helplessness, self-worth motivation and mastery orientation. The eighth item focused on peer esteem, asking if the child maintained 'her/his position in the eyes of (some) other pupils by not taking work seriously, and not being seen to make much effort'. Finally, there was a global question about motivation: 'Is (he/she) a child I find difficult or impossible to motivate?' Each item was rated on a four-point scale.

Teachers were asked to complete two separate questionnaires for each pupil, one tapping the class teacher's perceptions of their pupils' motivational style and ability in English, and the other in Mathematics. The reason for separate questionnaires in these two subjects was to investigate the possibility that subject context might be an additional influence on motivational style, over and above that of the pupil's ability or behaviour. Apart from this, the two questionnaires were identical. In addition we obtained Standardised Reading Test Scores based on either a Macmillan (1985) or Burt (1974) Reading Test.

Differences between English and Mathematics

We compared the mean (average) rating for each item in English with that in mathematics. The results revealed only two items in which the difference between the means was statistically significant. Children were significantly more likely to be rated as under-achieving in English than in mathematics, and the same was true of peer esteem ('maintains his her position in the eyes of (some) other pupils by not taking work seriously and not being seen to make much effort'). Although no significant differences were found in the other items, these results were interesting at two levels. First, mathematics is widely thought to be a difficult subject to teach, but the teachers in our survey seemed to see greater problems with English. If teachers expect less of their pupils in mathematics than in English, because they themselves find it difficult, they may see under-achievement, defined in terms of performance relative to ability, as more prevalent in English. Second, these classes were typical of a majority of primary schools in that the class teacher taught almost all of the curriculum. With greater curriculum differentiation in secondary schools, including subject specialist teachers, differences between subjects in motivation or behaviour might be substantially greater.

Recognition of motivational style and relationship between motivational style and learning difficulties

These questions are related and we addressed them in two ways. First, we discussed each item with teachers at the planning stage. It was clear from these discussions that teachers could instantly think of children to whom each description applied. At this level, these motivational styles appeared to be meaningful. Next, we examined the relationships between each item and each of the other items. The resulting correlation matrix showed a strong positive relationship between maladaptive motivational styles and learning and behavioural difficulties. Although learned helplessness and self-worth motivation had a statistically significant relationship with troublesome classroom behaviour, the relationship between the latter and peer esteem was even stronger.

As expected, mastery orientation was negatively correlated with maladaptive motivational styles. However, the strong relationship between learned helplessness and self-worth motivation suggested that although teachers could distinguish quite easily between the broader categories of adaptive and maladaptive motivational styles they had greater difficulty in distinguishing between these two maladaptive styles.

The latter finding is of some importance. In theory, saying to a learned helpless child 'this may be difficult' will merely confirm the child's view that there is no point in attempting the task: 'if even the teacher says it's difficult, there's obviously no point in trying'. In contrast, saying the same thing to a self-worth motivated child may have the reverse effect: 'if even the teacher says it's difficult, nobody will think I'm stupid if I can't do it'. In practice, very little is known about how children interpret remarks which their teachers intend as encouraging. We cannot assume they will interpret encouragement or feedback in the way we intend.

Do teachers identify equal numbers of boys and girls?

In keeping with almost all other studies we found that boys were significantly more likely than girls to be seen as under-achieving and displaying troublesome classroom behaviour (e.g. Rutter *et al.*, 1970, 1979). What was perhaps more interesting was that:

- boys were significantly more likely to be seen as difficult or impossible to motivate;
- girls were rated significantly higher than boys on the mastery oriented item;
- in relation to maladaptive motivational styles, boys were rated significantly higher on learned helplessness, self-worth motivation and peer esteem.

The high proportion of mastery oriented girls is consistent with a growing body of evidence that girls outperform boys in almost every subject of the National Curriculum at least until GCSE. The gender bias in teachers' perceptions raises some interesting questions, including whether boys will see themselves as less highly motivated to succeed at school. Nevertheless even if this could be shown to be the case it would not follow that boys were less highly motivated to succeed than girls in out of school tasks. In this connection, it is worth noting that although teachers are more likely to identify boys as presenting behaviour problems than girls, this is not the case when parents are the informants (Rutter *et al.*, 1970).

Differences between teachers

We compared the mean scores of the six teachers on each item and found highly significant differences between them in their ratings of troublesome behaviour. Two teachers reported unusually high rates, and one an exceptionally low rate. We did not, however, find differences between teachers in their ratings of motivational style.

Conclusions from teachers' assessments of motivational style

The results of this small-scale investigation confirm other evidence that teachers regard a large minority of pupils as presenting learning and/or behavioural difficulties (e.g. DES, 1978; SED, 1978). School and teacher effectiveness research shows significant differences between schools, and between teachers within a school, in pupils' behaviour (e.g. Mortimore *et al.*, 1988). Findings from this project confirm such differences, at least in relation to teachers' perceptions. In addition we found that teachers' perceptions of troublesome behaviour were related to their perceptions of motivational style. In other words, teachers perceived children with learning or behavioural difficulties as having a maladaptive motivational style.

It follows that these teachers' conceptions of motivation were not simply quantitative as implied by descriptions such as 'unmotivated' or 'low in motivation' but rather that their conceptions were qualitative in nature. They did not, however, appear to distinguish between the maladaptive styles of learned helplessness, self-worth motivation and peer esteem. It seems unlikely that this was simply a function of the instrument, since prior discussions with teachers had confirmed that the questions were clear and meaningful. It seems more likely that in large primary classes teachers cannot easily distinguish between different maladaptive styles.

If so, there is the possibility of a mismatch between the teacher's perceptions of a child and the child's attributions of the causes of her or his difficulties. In turn, this raises questions about the role of gender in motivational style. In keeping with other studies boys were substantially over-represented both in learning and in behaviour difficulties; girls were significantly more likely to be rated as mastery orientated but boys as showing a maladaptive motivational style. The experimental literature shows a tendency for girls with maladaptive style to be identified as learned helpless, and for boys with a maladaptive style to be identified as self-worth motivated (e.g. Craske, 1988). Teachers' assessments in our study could have been affected by at least two sources of bias. First, it is clear from other work that girls are less likely than boys to behave disruptively. This is not just a question of teachers' perceptions (e.g. Rutter *et al.*, 1979). Because boys are more likely to disturb the routine of the classroom, teachers may give them high ratings of maladaptive motivational style, but because the class is large they cannot easily distinguish between reasons for maladaptive motivation. Second, the first four items focused on learning and behavioural difficulties, and this could have predisposed teachers to concentrate on pupils presenting these difficulties when answering the questions on motivational style. As we noted earlier, evidence from pupils themselves might provide a different picture, whether based on their responses to classroom tasks or their answers to a questionnaire.

The results of the English and mathematics questionnaires raise similar questions. The only gender differences were related to under-achievement and to peer esteem. In each case the evidence indicated greater problems in English than in mathematics. The study of teachers' perceptions obviously tells us nothing about pupils' responses. Nevertheless, the evidence suggests that we should not assume that there will be no consistent differences in children's motivation in the various subjects of the National Curriculum. Not only may teaching methods vary from subject to subject, but teaching method may be influenced by the content and structure of the curriculum. For their part, pupils may respond to their perceptions of content and/or teaching methods.

Potential influences on motivational style: priorities for research

Based on our discussion so far, we propose three groups of influences on motivational style as a priority for further investigation. These arise partly from the study of teacher assessments and partly from the literature reviewed in Chapter 2. They distinguish explicitly between characteristics of the pupils themselves and characteristics of their school and classroom experience. As such, we are clearly working with an interactive model of motivational style. We see motivation as the product of an interaction between factors in the pupils themselves and aspects of their environment.

Gender, ability and age

We have already commented on gender as a potential influence on motivational style. Ability raises more complex questions. There is a powerful argument for focusing on ability as perceived by pupils themselves and by their teachers. Nicholls' (1989) work on the development of children's concepts of ability and Dweck's (1985) on the distinction between incremental and entity concepts of ability suggest that this could be useful. Our principal interest, though, was not to disentangle the complex notion of ability but rather to provide solid empirical evidence about the motivation of pupils who are difficult to teach. This suggested the need for a different approach. In our project on teachers' assessments of motivational style we distinguished between children of low ability and children who were under-achieving. The former would have low educational attainments but would not be under-achieving. There is no prima facie reason why they should be any more likely to show a maladaptive style than educationally successful children at the top of the attainment range. In contrast, the under-achievers probably would be expected to show a maladaptive style.

We can only know whether maladaptive motivational styles are disproportionately represented in pupils with special needs if we know their prevalence in a representative group of all pupils. Hence, any project on the prevalence of motivational styles in pupils with special needs must address their prevalence in the full ability range. A related question is whether maladaptive motivational styles become more or less prevalent with age, either amongst pupils with learning difficulties or other pupils. Nicholls' (1989) views on the development of children's concept of ability suggest that an increasingly stable view of ability develops in adolescence. If so, pupils will be more likely to attribute failure to a stable cause over which they have no control, and we should expect to see an age-related increase in maladaptive styles. To investigate this it will clearly be necessary to compare responses of different year groups.

Subject, teacher and school influences

Elsewhere Galloway (1995) has argued that home and social background factors are the principal influences on truancy, and also on delinquency. In contrast, the teacher is the principal influence on pupils' behaviour within the classroom and the social climate or ethos of the school on their behaviour elsewhere in the school (e.g. in the playground and between lessons). School factors are also paramount in exclusion from school, though not the same factors as operate within the classroom. It follows that in looking for motivational influences one should include the school and the teachers. For reasons explained earlier, we also need to take account of possible differences between subjects as an influence on motivational style.

Investigating the possibility of school, teacher and subject influences on motivation has substantial implications for methodology. It implies the need for comparison between schools and teachers, and hence for a larger sample. While much can be gained from a small-scale experimental study, or from an intensive observation- and interview-based study of one or two classes, different methods are needed to investigate the possibility that schools as social organisations or teachers as individuals exert an important influence on their pupils' motivation.

Transfer from primary to secondary school

An enormous amount of time and effort is expended each year in preparing pupils to transfer to secondary school. There is some evidence that spending a day attending classes is more helpful than more formal visits (Delamont and Galton, 1986). Nevertheless, the evidence suggests that pupils' progress tends to slow down in their first year in secondary school and also that their motivation is adversely affected (see Chapter 6). Any project which includes school and teacher influences and crosses the primary–secondary divide suggests the value of following pupils from their final year in primary school to their first year in secondary.

Investigating motivational style

Underlying requirements

In planning our own work we were influenced by three considerations. First, while information from teachers was valuable it was no substitute for information from pupils themselves. Second, we needed to obtain information about children's actual responses to tasks in which motivation was important, and as far as possible these should be with familiar tasks and in familiar settings. In other words, it would not be adequate to confine ourselves to a questionnaire study which sought pupils' *perceptions* of how they would feel or behave in different situations. Third, because we were interested principally in pupils with learning and/or behavioural difficulties our conception of motivation should be one which focused on responses to tasks which pupils might find difficult. Mastery orientation implies that pupils are not deterred from future effort by the experience of failure; rather they see how they can overcome the problem.

These assumptions raise a question about the potential distinction between cognitive and behavioural measures of motivation. To explain this it is useful to consider the relationships between attitudes and behaviour. Although teachers often use attitude as synonymous for behaviour, for example in comments like 'he/she's got an appalling attitude', the relationship is by no means clear. Attitudes are not always reflected in behaviour, nor vice versa. Thus, some people have racist attitudes but include people of a different ethnic group amongst their friends. Conversely it is possible to hold liberal and 'politically correct' attitudes, yet strenuously avoid any contact with people of a different ethnic group. Similarly, it does not follow that evidence of high motivation from a questionnaire will be reflected in actual behaviour when confronted with a particular difficult task in the classroom.

Assessing motivational style in the classroom

Given the underlying requirements just mentioned, we had to find a way of obtaining behaviour-based information about motivational style from a large number of pupils in the natural setting of primary and secondary school classrooms. Our first concern was to obtain evidence based on pupils' actual reactions, not just evidence based on questionnaire responses. Since direct observation was ruled out by the need to obtain information across age groups, classes and subjects, our options were somewhat limited. There was, however, one technique which would distinguish between mastery orientation, learned helplessness and self-worth motivation. This was developed by Craske (1988). She designed four tests, A, B, C and D, in which tests A, C and D were of equal difficulty but Test B was significantly more difficult. After each test children were told their scores on the previous test(s). Children who did as well or better on Test C as on Test A were identified as mastery oriented on the grounds that their performance had not been adversely affected by their lower score on the more difficult Test B. Children who obtained a lower score on Test C than on Test A were identified as showing a maladaptive motivational style as their performance on Test C had apparently been adversely affected by their lower score on Test B. Before Test D children were told that they might find it difficult. Children whose score deteriorated on Test D by comparison with Test C were identified as learned helpless on the ground that 'giving up' when told the test might be difficult could be interpreted as evidence of lack of confidence in their own ability. Children whose scores improved on Test D by comparison with Test C, or remained the same, were defined as self-worth motivated on the grounds that because a teacher had defined the task as difficult, failure need not be attributed to lack of ability.

Craske's technique met a number of our requirements. It was a behavioural measure of motivation, and distinguished in a coherent, logical way between the principal motivational styles in which we were interested. In particular, it met the requirement of focusing our motivational responses on responses to a task which children would be likely to find difficult.

It also contained three principal problems. First, Craske developed her technique for experimental research to investigate the effects of attribution retraining on learned helpless and self-worth motivated children. Consequently, the tests she developed would not be suitable for our purposes in mainstream primary and secondary school classrooms. Second, we have already noted the difficulty with the concept of self-worth motivation (p. 36) and there was no obvious way of refining the concept in Craske's technique to distinguish between pupils motivated principally by anxiety about their own ability and pupils motivated principally by the need to retain their status with their peers. Finally, the statistical basis for the technique is questionable. However similar two or more versions of the same test may be, there is inevitably some variation in pupils' performance. This 'standard error' of each test could result in some children doing better, or worse, on Test C by comparison with Test A, quite independently of the motivational influence of the more difficult Test B. Specialist statistical advice indicated, however, that Craske's diagnostic procedure was acceptable provided we used it to show general patterns of motivational style in selected groups of children, for example pupils in different ability groups. This, of course, is quite different from using it to assess individual pupils in clinical practice or educational assessment purposes.

Given the scale of our proposed project the third of these problems did not apply; we did not intend to carry out clinical research. The problem of inability to distinguish between anxiety about ability and about peer esteem could, in principle, be reduced by interviewing selected pupils about their motivational responses. Design of suitable tests would undoubtedly be time consuming, but not impossibly so provided we kept them short, and with a limited focus. We therefore decided to adapt Craske's technique for use with pupils in mainstream primary and secondary schools.

Other measures of motivation

While our principal interest was in a behaviour-based measure of motivation, we were also interested in whether other measures would provide a similar picture. We have already mentioned Nicholls' (1989) distinction between task orientation, ego orientation and work avoidance. His motivational orientation scales were designed with these distinctions in mind. In preparing them for pupils' use we renamed them as a 'What I think of school' questionnaire in order to make them more user-friendly, and we have retained this title throughout the book. Similarly, we have mentioned DeCharms' (1976) distinction between 'origin' and 'pawn' measures of motivation. His Origin Climate questionnaire enabled us to obtain information on these. We designated this as the 'My Class in School' questionnaire when we asked pupils to complete it.

Pupils, motivational style and the curriculum: a curriculum-focused study

Selecting a sample

Having decided at least on the outline of our approach we had to decide on the scope of the study. This was dictated by the funds and time available. Two comprehensive secondary schools in the North of England agreed to take part in the project, together with 11 of their principal feeder primary schools. Springtown School served a fairly affluent suburban catchment area with mainly owner-occupied houses and fewer than five per cent ethnic minority pupils. Summertown School served an urban area with a high rate of social disadvantage and over 50 per cent of pupils of Asian origin. This provided an additional dimension to the project, enabling us to compare the motivational styles of pupils of Asian and European origin.

We tested all 530 pupils in their final term of primary schooling. Of these 228 transferred either to Springtown or to Summertown School and formed a longitudinal sample for comparison between the final year of primary and the first year of secondary school. As well as testing these pupils again in the first term of Year 7, we also included other new entrants to the two secondary schools, making a total of 437. Extending the longitudinal sample into the later years of secondary schooling was impractical. We therefore included all available pupils in Year 9 (aged 13–14) and Year 11 (aged 15–16) totalling 389 and 380 respectively. Only pupils who completed all four tests of the Craske instrument could be included in the results. Since testing took place on four separate days, sometimes with an intervening week-end, this resulted in a considerable reduction in sample size, from approximately 22 per cent in Year 6 to 37 per cent in Year 7.

Test construction

We developed the English and mathematics tests for each of the four age groups, Years 6, 7, 9 and 11, in consultation with teachers in the participating primary and secondary schools. With their agreement, we adapted items for the mathematics tests from published schemes of work with which pupils would be familiar. The tests covered aspects of arithmetic, algebra and geometry but did not cover investigative or exploratory mathematics. This was due to the constraint that we could allow only 15 minutes for each test.

For the English tests, pupils were asked to read a passage of prose and then answer questions based on it. The questions were designed to test their understanding of the passage, both at the level of factual information and the underlying meaning. For primary pupils, passages were selected from books suited to their age and ability, and for secondary from a well-known published scheme (SRA, 1970) with the proviso that pupils had not previously used the selected passages in class.

The tests had to be suitable for use by the full ability range of pupils in each year group. Following discussion with teachers we designed test batteries in each subject at two difficulty levels for Year 6, three difficulty levels for Year 7, four for Year 9 and for Year 11 three difficulty levels in English and four in mathematics. We thus had a total of 12 test batteries in English and 13 in mathematics.

Each test battery had to contain English or mathematics tasks which would be reasonably familiar to pupils. In addition, tests A, C and D had to be easy enough for pupils to have a realistic aim of tackling several items successfully, but not so easy that little effort was required. At the planning and piloting stages we encountered a tendency on the part of some teachers to underestimate their pupils' capabilities. Thus, some pupils who had been selected on the basis of school records and advice from teachers to take the lowest difficulty level were in fact capable of the intermediate level. An acceptable difficulty level was nevertheless achieved for most pupils. Test results were standardised on a 10-point scale. In 17 of the 25 test batteries the mean score on Test A ranged from 5.0 to 8.0 and in 24 out of 25 between 4.2 and 8.3. The aberrant result was 3.4 in the least difficult mathematics test for Year 7. In all but three cases the standard deviation was below 2.5 and in these three the highest was 2.87 In every case results confirmed that Test B was more difficult than Test A. It was nevertheless clear that most pupils had attempted at least some of the questions successfully. The only exceptions were the lower ability pupils in mathematics in Year 11, where there was evidence of refusal to attempt the difficult task even though they had scored 50 per cent on Test A.

Interview schedules

In addition to the questionnaires from Nicholls (1989) and DeCharms (1976) we recognised the need for more qualitative information from pupils about their attributions for success or failure. In particular, we wanted to find out more about their perceptions of the curriculum tests and about their 'metaperceptions', i.e. their beliefs about what other people, particularly teachers, were expecting of them. We were only able to interview a minority of pupils, but included children showing each of the motivational styles identified by Craske's technique. We will give further details about these interviews in Chapter 7.

Identification of special educational needs

We had access to standardised test scores for pupils in the longitudinal sample and Year 9 (Thorndike *et al.*, 1986; Moray House, 1982). These gave information on pupils' non-verbal reasoning ability, which we used as a measure of cognitive ability. They also contained measures described as verbal and quantitative reasoning which provided a useful measure of pupils' attainments in English and in Mathematics. For Year 11 pupils we relied on GCSE examination results. In each case, attainment and cognitive ability scores were standardised to a mean of 100 (standard deviation 15) and allocated to one of four bands, Band 1: >115, Band 2: 100–114; Band 3: 85–99; Band 4: <85.

Conclusions

This chapter has outlined the results of a small-scale project on primary teachers' assessments of their pupils' motivational styles. We used these, together with the literature covered in Chapter 2 to propose a number of priorities for further research. We argued that this should include a behavioural measure of motivational style and summarised the methods we used to collect information. In Chapters 4–7 we will outline the results and discuss their possible implications.

PART TWO

Influences on motivation

CHAPTER FOUR

Ability and attainment, race and gender

Introduction

Running across all the differing models of the motivational process, reviewed in Chapter 2, is the common assumption that motivational characteristics will interact with other relatively stable characteristics, for example, gender. In as much as these other characteristics have an influence on personality, the patterns of information concerning past performance available to the individual or the goals that a person might be working to, then there ought to be some association between these characteristics and the motivational patterns displayed. In Chapter 2 we noted Atkinson's claim that motivational characteristics were primarily a function of basic personality traits and the expectations people have for success in a given achievement-related situation. The personality traits in question concern a capacity for anxiety in relation to failure and a capacity for positive emotional responses in relation to success. It is often claimed that girls are more likely than boys to experience anxiety in relation to mathematics. If this is accepted as a general trait related to gender, and in turn is associated with the anxiety states relevant to Atkinson's theory, then girls ought to demonstrate more maladaptive motivational responses to mathematics than boys.

Clearly, a number of assumptions are being made here and a more substantial case would be needed before they could be fully accepted. However, the critical point is that it is frequently assumed that motivational patterns are influenced by stable characteristics of the individual such as gender. One issue to be explored in this chapter is whether the evidence we have gathered offers any support for this assumption. The importance for teachers is obvious: can they realistically hope to encourage positive motivation in their pupils, or are the dominant influences beyond their control?

Our research examined the effects of intellectual ability and gender together with ethnicity on the prevalence of motivational style. Our overarching preoccupation was with the motivation of the 'difficult to teach'. It is widely accepted that groups of pupils identified in terms of their non-verbal reasoning, their educational attainments, their gender and their ethnicity may be difficult to teach. It is perfectly reasonable therefore to assume that in certain areas at least, pupils defined in these ways will have motivational problems.

The opposing assumption is not, of course, that pupils classified in these ways will not have motivational difficulties, but that any difficulties experienced will not be a function of the classification itself. That is low ability pupils, or pupils of one gender, when they do display maladaptive motivational styles do not do so because of their gender or ability levels *per se*, but due to other factors prevalent at the time.

We shall proceed to examine the influence of ability levels and gender together with ethnic grouping using Craske's (1988) technique to assess motivational style in aspects of English and mathematics. We shall also draw upon the measures of motivational orientation derived from the work of Nicholls (1989).

Ability and attainment

The first claim that we wish to explore is that less able pupils have less adaptive motivational patterns than the more able. In her book, Deborah Stipek (1993) describes a number of student types. Each of these is held to represent a particularly problematic case in terms of motivational characteristics. Stipek's 'Hopeless Hannah' is of interest to us here. Hannah has little confidence in her ability. She is a student with a history of a low level of performance in a number of areas of the curriculum. Above all else, Hannah is seen to be a student who will not try to overcome difficulties and is highly resistant to the teacher's attempts to enthuse or motivate her. Readers of earlier parts of this book will recognise even in this briefest of descriptions the characteristics of the learned helpless child. Stipek describes this as 'the motivational problem most resistant to change by even the most clever and persistent teacher' and the consequences of the problem as 'devastating'. It is clear from Stipek's account that helplessness is regarded as being associated with actual low level of ability. Stipek's own view of the dynamics of helplessness bear most resemblance to the information processing view of motivational style set out in Chapter 2. As a result of poor levels of actual performance, relative to classmates, helpless pupils increasingly come to expect failure. In line with this they also come increasingly to understand their own failures in terms which further endorse low expectations. The Hannahs of this world get trapped.

Accounts of this sort give rise to two assumptions about the relationship between ability, performance levels and motivational style. The first is that maladaptive motivational style and perhaps learned helplessness in particular will be associated with low intellectual ability and/or low attainments. This is an assumption which we can address fairly directly. It is an issue of prevalence. The view outlined by Stipek, and held by many others, is not that all lower ability and low attainment children will show maladaptive motivational styles. Neither, of course, is it that all children with maladaptive motivational styles will be of low ability and/or experience low levels of performance. Rather the claim is that lower ability and lower attainment groups will be more likely to demonstrate maladaptive motivational styles.

The second assumption implicit in the account of Stipek is a more complex one. Rather than being concerned with the issue of prevalence, this is concerned with the issue of causality. In virtually any area of research it is more difficult to establish clear evidence regarding causality than it is to demonstrate the relative prevalence of phenomena. However, let us examine in a little more detail the claims regarding causality that Stipek is implying. A circular, or feedback loop, notion of causality is being invoked. In describing the helpless child she states that: 'Because they rarely try, they rarely succeed.' The lack of effort is a function of the individual's motivational style. She also says: 'Their repeated failures confirm their perceptions of themselves as incompetent.' In other words, actual performance produces low expectations which are themselves part of the individual's motivational style.

In terms of the data available to us here this leads to two testable predictions. The first is that pupils who have a lower level of measured educational achievement ought to be over-represented in the maladaptive motivational categories. The second is that those with lower levels of measured cognitive ability ought to appear more often in the maladaptive motivational categories.

These two predictions are not the same, although they are clearly related. The difference between the two is important. A measured association between achievement and motivation tells us nothing about causality. The circularity highlighted by Stipek assumes a relationship between achievement and motivation. However, the simple observation of such a relationship could support a circular notion of causality: low achievement could cause low motivation, *or* vice versa. A known relationship with a measure of intelligence, however, is a little different. In this case, it is difficult to accept a model of causality which posits low motivation as the cause and low intelligence as the effect.

The effect of intelligence, attainment, gender and ethnicity

As described earlier, we had data on non-verbal reasoning ability and on attainment in English and mathematics. The information available within schools was inevitably variable, but Year 7 schools were able to provide a virtually complete set of NFER Cognitive Ability Tests (Thorndike *et al.*, 1986). These tests produce scores for non-verbal reasoning (NVR), verbal reasoning (VR), and quantitative reasoning (QR). The verbal and quantitative reasoning tests measure aspects of a pupil's ability in English and mathematics respectively and are known to correlate highly with measures of attainment in these subjects. Hence verbal reasoning was taken as a measure of achievement in English, quantitative reasoning as a measure of achievement in mathematics, and non-verbal reasoning as a measure of cognitive ability relating to both subjects.

For Year 9 the data set was less complete, with full information available only in relation to motivational styles in English and Mathematics and a VR measure of English achievement. For Year 11 we had access to GCSE scores. These were available for English and Mathematics, and we also had the overall performance of each pupil at GCSE. These scores enabled us to examine the relationships between motivational style and a clearly highly important aspect of performance.

Motivational style, ability and attainment: children's responses to curriculum tasks

Tables 4.1 and 4.2 set out the relationships for Year 7 between the NFER measure of cognitive ability and the categories of motivational style in English and in mathematics as produced by the Craske procedure. The main interest here is in the relationship between motivational style, as assessed by the Craske technique, and the pupils' measured levels of NVR. Pupils are allocated to one of four attainment bands. Following convention these bands are determined by the normal distribution of scores, with a mean of 100 and a standard deviation of 15. Hence Band 1 pupils, those with the highest measured level of achievement, are those who have a score of 115 or above. The bottom band pupils, Band 4, are those with a score less than 85.

In relation to English, first of all, the results in Table 4.1 show significant differences between bands for mastery orientation and learned helplessness. Combining boys and girls, Band 1 pupils are significantly more likely to be mastery oriented than Band 4. Moreover, there is a steady decrease in the percentage of pupils appearing in the mastery orientation category as one moves from Band 1 to Band 4. In short, more intelligent children in Year 7 as measured by a non-verbal reasoning test, are more likely to display mastery orientation. When the data are examined separately for each gender it can be seen that this effect is much more prominent in boys than in girls. Band 4 boys are less

Table 4.1 Cognitive ability (non-verbal reasoning) in four bands, gender and motivational style in English in Year 7 (N=272)

Motivational style		Band 1 (≥115) N=27 %	Band 2 (100–114) N=99 %	Band 3 (85–99) N=85 %	Band 4 (<85) N=61 %	LLR† df=3	Sub-groups df=3
	Boys N	14	58	38	47		
	Girls N	13	41	47	14		
	*						
Mastery oriented	Boys	42.9	32.8	36.8	10.6	11.91 p<0.01	4<3: p<0.05
	N	6	19	14	5		4<1: p<.05
	Girls	46.2	31.7	14.9	28.6	6.53 NS	
	N	6	13	7	4		
	All	44.4	32.3	24.7	14.8	10.62 p<0.01	4<1: p<.01
	N	12	32	21	9		
Learned helplessness	Boys	28.6	44.8	85.0	61.6	5.87 NS	
	N	4	26	19	29		
	Girls	30.8	48.8	59.6	50.0	3.65 NS	
	N	4	20	28	7		
	All	29.6	46.5	55.3	59.0	8.04 p<0.05	NS
	N	8	46	47	36		
Self-worth motivation	Boys	28.6	22.4	13.2	27.7	3.11 NS	
	N	4	13	5	13		
	Girls	23.1	19.5	25.5	21.4	0.47 NS	
	N	3	8	12	3		
	All	25.9	21.2	20	26.2	1.05 NS	
	N	7	21	17	16		

* Percentage of children with motivational style in band.
† Log likelihood ratio. (This test of statistical significance has the technical advantage of coherence over the more familiar chisquare; if the overall result for the four bands is not significant, it is mathematically impossible for any of the sub-groups to differ to a significant degree.)

Table 4.2 Cognitive ability (non-verbal reasoning) in four bands, gender and motivational style in mathematics in Year 7 (N=304)

Motivational style		Band 1 (>115) N=26 16 10 %	Band 2 (100–114) N=117 71 46 %	Band 3 (85–99) N=93 49 44 %	Band 4 (<85) N=68 51 17 %	LLR† df=3	Sub-groups df=3
	Boys N / Girls N / *						
Mastery oriented	Boys	50.0	47.9	40.8	33.3	3.05	
	N	8	34	20	17	NS	
	Girls	50.0	58.7	43.2	11.8	12.44	4<2: p<0.01
	N	5	27	19	2	p<0.006	
	All	50.0	52.1	41.9	27.9	11.07	4<2: p<0.02
	N	13	61	39	19	p<0.01	
Learned helplessness	Boys	25.0	29.6	34.7	29.4	0.691	
	N	4	21	17	15	NS	
	Girls	30.0	17.4	27.3	70.6	15.89	4>3: p<0.05
	N	3	8	12	12	p<0.002	4>2: p<0.01
	All	26.9	24.8	31.2	39.7	4.64	
	N	7	29	29	27	NS	
Self-worth motivation	Boys	25.0	22.5	24.5	37.3	3.48	
	N	4	16	12	19	NS	
	Girls	20.0	23.9	29.5	17.6	1.16	
	N	2	11	13	3	NS	
	All	23.1	23.1	26.9	32.4	2.03	
	N	6	27	25	22	NS	

* Percentage of children with motivational style in band.
† Log likelihood ratio.

likely to demonstrate mastery orientation in response to a difficult task. There is still a tendency for higher band girls to be more likely to show mastery orientation but the effect is not strong enough to reach statistical significance.

Given this, we might expect lower band pupils to be more likely to display one of the maladaptive motivational styles. The overall trend within learned helplessness supports this with a significant tendency for pupils to show learned helplessness in response to a difficult task as non-verbal reasoning decreases. This trend is broadly supported within each gender group, but the effect is not strong enough to reach significance in the statistical sense. There is no overall significant effect for the self-worth motive with the data for boys suggesting a curvilinear relationship (the high and low groups being more likely to display the self-worth motive).

Table 4.2 shows the same set of data, in respect to mathematics. The overall picture is broadly similar. Pupils in the lowest band are less likely to demonstrate mastery orientation and there is a tendency for them to be more likely to display learned helplessness. There are, again, no significant effects for the self-worth motive. However, it is important to note that whereas in English Band 4 boys were less likely to show mastery orientation than girls, in mathematics the reverse applies. So here we see girls being particularly less likely to display mastery orientation in mathematics if they are in the bottom band (only 2 out of 17 girls do) and it is low band girls (12 out of 17) who are most likely to display the learned helpless response. The influence of gender on motivational style will be returned to later in this chapter, but we have here evidence to support the view that a low level of non-verbal reasoning has a greater impact on girls' motivation in mathematics, but a greater influence on boys' motivation in English.

The overall conclusion then, is that a measure of non-verbal reasoning does have a bearing on motivational style. A positive form of motivation is more likely to be displayed by the higher band pupils, while learned helplessness is particularly associated with pupils in the lowest band. In as much as non-verbal reasoning is a measure of underlying intelligence rather than subject-specific performance, this finding offers some support to the view that motivational style will develop as a consequence of typical past performance levels, which themselves are partly determined by cognitive ability.

The pattern of results for the measures of English and mathematics attainment and the associated patterns of motivational style were broadly very similar (Galloway *et al.*, 1995). In English the lowest attainment band pupils showed less mastery orientation, with this effect being particularly clear for boys. Low attaining pupils were more likely to display the learned helpless response in English. For mathematics, mastery orientation was less likely to be a feature of the responses of the lowest attainment pupils, particularly for girls, and the lowest attainment band of girls were especially prone to learned helplessness. We also found here, for the first time, an effect for the self-worth motive. Boys in Band 4 were more likely than boys in any of the other bands to display the self-worth motive in mathematics.

For Year 7, both in relation to non-verbal reasoning as well as to subject-specific measures of attainment there was a clear association between attainment and motivational style. While there was some evidence of a general trend towards less adaptive styles as achievements decreased, the data more readily support the view that it was pupils in the lowest achievement band who were more likely to experience maladaptive forms of motivation than any of their peers.

The data for Year 9 were less complete. Verbal reasoning data were available for both secondary schools, but the quantitative and non-verbal ability data were only available for one of the two schools. However, examination of the English/verbal ability material allowed a comparison with the findings for Year 7.

The principal difference between Years 7 and 9 Craske style and English achievement relates to the particular maladaptive style adopted by the lower-achieving pupils. In Year 7 the trend is for lower band pupils to be under-represented in the mastery orientation category, but over-represented in the learned helplessness category. In Year 9 the trend is for the same under-representation in mastery orientation, but for the over-representation to be found in the self-worth motive rather than learned helplessness. It is worth recalling that much of the work by Covington and his colleagues which led to the current formulation of the self-worth motive was based on data obtained from more mature students at college level.

We will now turn to the Year 11 data to see how these relationships operate in relation to our most educationally significant measure, GCSE scores. Reflecting the historic development of the GCSE examinations from O levels and CSEs, it is customary to regard a pass at grade C or better as representing a benchmark to indicate the potential for A level study. In the following analysis this broad distinction between C+ grade passes and grades below C is maintained. The question we asked was whether the level of GCSE grade obtained in English and in mathematics reflected the pupils' motivational style as measured by the Craske procedure.

The answer was quite clear. Motivational style as measured by the Craske technique did not relate to GCSE performance. While maladaptive motivational styles were clearly related to low cognitive ability and low attainments, as shown by the Years 7 and 9 data, no such relationship was evident from the GCSE results. Examination of the available data separately for each GCSE grade also showed no clear signs of an association between Craske style and performance. That is, those obtaining grade As or grade Fs were not likely to differ in terms of motivational style.

In considering the pattern of results in different age groups it has to be recognised that the data available to us are based on non-verbal reasoning, a measure of English attainment and a measure of mathematics attainment in Year 7, a measure of English attainment in Year 9 and GCSE scores in Year 11. However, it is not clear why motivational style should be related to non-verbal reasoning and attainment in Years 7 and 9 but not in Year 11. The underlying constructs are the same across the age groups. However, the achievement measures in Years 7 and 9 were based on results from 'one-off' tests (Thorndike *et al.*, 1986), whereas the GCSE results represented the culmination of two years' work, including a substantial amount of assessed coursework. As such, one might reasonably expect a different set of motivational principles to apply to GCSE results than to measures of non-verbal reasoning and measures of educational achievement based on 'one-off' tests.

Further light may be shed on this by turning attention to the second measure of motivational style available to us. This measure draws upon the work of Nicholls (1989) and his colleagues and involves a different way of investigating motivational style or, in Nicholls' terms, the motivational orientation of pupils.

Motivational style, ability and attainment: pupils' responses to Nicholls' motivational orientation scale

Craske's technique is a measure of motivational style based on pupils' actual responses to a sequence of tests. It tells us how they responded, but does not tell us how they felt about their work in English and in mathematics. To investigate this we used Nicholls' (1989) Motivational Orientation Scale. In essence, this is a 16-item instrument designed to distinguish between the motivational styles or, in Nicholls' terms, 'orientations' of task orientation, ego orientation and work avoidance (see p. 32). Our first task was to use the statistical technique of principal components analysis to identify 'factors', or groups of items which pupils had answered in a similar way. The results confirmed that responses of pupils in our sample followed the same pattern as in Nicholls' North American samples: in other words we identified the same three factors (see Appendix A in Nicholls, 1989). We were then able to use these as sub-scales, to compare the mean ratings of items, for example for boys and girls, or for pupils in each of the four ability or attainment bands, and for pupils obtaining a GCSE grade of C or above and below grade C in each subject.

In English we found no difference between the four bands on task orientation. In contrast, in mathematics in Year 7 the highest achievement band had the highest level of task orientation. In Year 11 a similar effect is found for the difference between level of GCSE pass. Pupils with grade C and above had significantly higher levels of task orientation than did those with lower grade passes.

Ego orientation showed a wider range of significant effects. In English in both Years 7 and 9, the tendency was for lower attainment bands to show less ego orientation, this being particularly so for Band 4 in Year 7 and both Bands 3 and 4 in Year 9. In mathematics there was a similar effect with lower ability bands in Year 7 showing less ego orientation. This was also the case for GCSE performance, with the pupils with lower grades having less ego orientation.

Work avoidance produced fewer differences between bands. Only in English for Year 9 do the observed differences reach statistically significant levels with the lower attainment bands generally showing less work avoidance, perhaps because these pupils do not feel themselves to be under great pressure to succeed at school, and thus feel no great need to be active in avoiding work.

The overall effect was for the higher bands generally to show more task and more ego orientation, with minimal effects for work avoidance. While the Craske measure showed no significant association with performance in GCSE, Nicholls' measure shows a significant association between maladaptive motivational style and lower bands in mathematics and to a lesser extent in English.

To summarise, pupils' underlying level of achievement does relate to their motivational style. This is most clearly shown by the use of the Craske measure. Pupils' performance in GCSE examinations, representing the culmination of work carried out over a two-year period, is more likely to show an association with Nicholls' motivational orientations, but in mathematics only. The Craske measure of motivational style, while showing clear associations with measures of intelligence and of attainment in Years 7 and 9, does not relate to GCSE performance in Year 11. In contrast, Nicholls' scale, which gives us more information on how pupils feel about the curriculum, does indicate a statistically significant relationship between higher GCSE grades and the obviously adaptive task orientation sub-scale.

Gender and ethnicity

The same procedures were used as for non-verbal reasoning and achievement. First we compared the number of boys and girls in each motivational style on the basis of curriculum testing in Craske's (1988) procedure. As it is often assumed that gender roles are more clearly and strictly defined in the UK Asian community we also examined gender in interaction with ethnic group.

The results showed that gender itself did not relate to motivational style. Combining all pupils in Years 7–11, there was no relationship between motivational style and gender.

The addition of the ethnicity variable did not have a very substantial impact upon this overall picture. When the three year-groups were examined together the data suggested that in respect of English there was an association between gender and motivational style for the Asian ethnic group. Asian girls were more likely to be included in the mastery orientation category than their male counterparts, while Asian males were more likely to be in the self-worth category. When each year group was examined separately there were no significant differences for Year 7 while the other year groups produced differences only with respect to English. In Year 11 Asian girls were more likely to appear in the mastery category than Asian males. For Year 9, Asian females were again more likely than their male counterparts to appear in the mastery category and Asian males were more likely to be in the self-worth motivated category than Asian females. Within the European group, boys were more likely than girls to be in the learned helpless category while girls were more likely than boys to be in the self-worth motivated category.

For gender, then, there were limited effects as far as motivational style defined by the Craske measure is concerned. There was some evidence of gender differences within ethnic groups but these were limited to English only. The consistent difference related to the tendency for Asian girls to be more mastery oriented than Asian boys with this difference appearing in both Years 9 and 11. The lack of any difference in Year 7 suggests that gender effects may become more important with age. However, even in the two older groups the effect is limited.

We also used the results from Nicholls' Motivational Orientation Scale to investigate the interaction between motivational orientation, gender and ethnicity. Overall, the data supported the view that girls were likely to have an advantage in terms of being more task oriented particularly in English. While they did not have more task orientation than boys in mathematics they did show an increase in task orientation in mathematics over the years of secondary schooling while males lost task orientation over the same period. Males had higher levels of ego orientation in both subject areas, implying that competition is more important to them than to the girls. Ethnicity and gender did not appear to interact with each other with respect to motivational orientations, but

European pupils seemed to be less task oriented in both subjects while Asians were more work avoidant in mathematics only.

The pattern supports many of the traditional views of the differences between girls and boys in respect to their motivation. Our evidence suggests that girls generally, and particularly in English, are likely to be more concerned with learning and with developing their understanding of the work they are engaged on. Boys, on the other hand, are more inclined to be driven by a concern to appear to be doing better than others. The literature on task and ego orientation would suggest that the girls would tend to be advantaged by the motivational patterns they display here, particularly perhaps by their tendency to increase in task orientation over the Years 7–11.

Finally it is worth reporting on the differences between the two genders in respect to actual GCSE performance. In both English and mathematics girls performed significantly better than boys. This is in line with current national trends. In English the mean difference here is equivalent to a grade, while in mathematics the difference is equivalent to approximately one-third of a grade. The greater advantage held by the girls in English quite possibly reflects their significantly higher levels of task orientation in this subject area.

Conclusions

To summarise the results from Nicholls' Motivational Orientation Scale first, there is a relationship between these measures and both non-verbal reasoning and attainment. The task orientation sub-scale relates to non-verbal reasoning and attainment only in mathematics with higher levels being found in the more able and the higher performers. Ego orientation has a somewhat wider influence, with higher levels being found amongst higher achieving pupils in both subjects and in the higher GCSE performers in mathematics. Work avoidance appears as the least important of the three orientations. These results provide further evidence of the importance of task orientation which, together with ego orientation is higher in mathematics than in English. This supports our general conclusion in Chapter 5 that English is a more problematic curriculum area from a motivational point of view than mathematics.

Ego orientation again relates to achievement and, in mathematics, to performance at GCSE: it is the higher band pupils who have the higher levels of ego orientation. High levels of ego orientation reflect satisfaction being gained from comparisons with others. These comparisons appear to be more important for those with high non-verbal reasoning or educational achievement scores. This finding confirms that enforced comparisons are likely to be particularly difficult for the less able to deal with.

With respect to gender differences, the most important effects are again in relation to task and ego orientation. Girls tend to have higher levels of task orientation, particularly in English, and perhaps more importantly they show an increase in task orientation over the years of secondary schooling. Boys tend to lose task orientation over this same period. With boys, the relative emphasis is more on ego orientation. In both subject areas it is boys who have significantly higher levels of ego orientation. The growing relative emphasis on task orientation for girls could well be associated with their higher levels of GCSE success. Girls' performance advantage is greater in English where they have the greater task orientation advantage. Boys' relative stress on ego orientation confirms the view that boys are more in tune with competitive and comparative educational environments. However, it should also be remembered that higher levels of ego orientation are not inimical to educational success.

The Craske measure of motivational style does not relate to GCSE performance, neither does it relate consistently to gender. In this case the association is with a measure of intelligence and measures of educational attainments. The essential finding is that pupils in the lowest band are less likely to display mastery orientation. Fuller discussion of the implications of this will follow at a later stage in this book. For the moment it can be suggested that the Craske measure is particularly sensitive to the motivational characteristics of pupils confronted with individual pieces of work which represent some type of test. The Craske tasks were designed to be like schoolwork. To a large degree they were. However, they could not be like the two-year long programme of work undertaken for GCSE. The Craske measure is more likely to reflect the ways in which a pupil responds when presented with a class test. The low band pupil, with a corresponding history of relatively low academic performance, is likely to enter into these tests with less confidence and hence to be more likely to display maladaptive forms of motivation in the test itself.

If this analysis is correct, the findings from our use of the Craske measure in relation to intelligence and educational achievement suggest that Band 4 pupils are doubly disadvantaged when confronted with test situations. Not only will their lower level of performance reduce their chances of success, but the motivational styles they are likely to adopt in such circumstances compound this. The maladaptive motivational responses they are likely to adopt prevent the full application of skills and knowledge they do possess. The lack of association between the Craske measure and the Year 11 performance on GCSE suggests that the coursework element and the longer time span involved reduce the chances of this form of 'test anxiety' having a negative impact.

At this stage, such conclusions are highly speculative. When the rest of our data have been presented we will be able to return to a broader discussion of the implications of these findings. The key point at the conclusion of this chapter is that it is not sufficient to ask questions about the motivation of particular groups of pupils. We need to ask questions about contextual influences, for example curriculum subject, school and teacher, as different motivational dynamics may apply in different circumstances. This is what we turn to in Chapter 5.

CHAPTER FIVE

Subject, school and teacher influences

Introduction

In Chapter 4 we showed a relationship between maladaptive motivational style and special educational need in Years 6, 7 and 9. By comparison, the effects of gender and ethnicity were relatively minor, at least on the behavioural measure of motivation based on Craske's technique. Yet although we found higher rates of maladaptive motivational style in Band 4 pupils, we did not find a steady increase from Band 1 to Band 4. Moreover, it is clear from Tables 4.1 and 4.2 that a substantial proportion of children with maladaptive motivational styles were not in Band 4. It is logical, therefore, to look for evidence of contextual influences on motivational style. Our research design enabled us to compare pupils' motivational responses to aspects of English and mathematics. It also enabled us to compare the responses of pupils in 11 primary schools and two secondary schools. Using the school data, it was also possible to compare the responses of pupils taught by different teachers. In this chapter, therefore, we will examine the evidence for differences in pupils' motivational styles arising from aspects of two curriculum areas, their school or their teacher. Showing the importance of these factors would further undermine approaches to motivation which emphasise the importance of a person's personality, and would strengthen the case for social-cognitive approaches which emphasise the pupils' responses to their experiences at school. We will not, however, be looking at the effect of transfer to secondary school, nor of increasing age, as both of these potentially powerful influences on motivational style are discussed in Chapter 6.

Why might school subject influence motivational style?

H.W. Marsh (1990) has provided convincing evidence about the existence of a distinctive self-concept in relation to different aspects of the self. One pupil may, for example, have a low self-concept in relation to her academic ability but a high self-concept in relation to her ability to make friends with other pupils of her own age. For another pupil the reverse may be the case. Global self-concept is, at best, of very limited usefulness, and at worst can be seriously misleading. Similarly, a measure of overall job satisfaction tells us nothing about which aspects of their job teachers find satisfying or, equally important, dissatisfying (Holdaway, 1978; Galloway *et al.*, 1985). Global measures of motivation have the same problem. The former Chief Medical Officer in the DES, Dr Kingsley Whitmore, once referred to the 'crude, naïve and lazy simplicity of terms like ESN and maladjusted'. These terms were, of course, abolished by the 1981 Education Act. There is an equally crude, naïve and lazy simplicity, though, in terms which remain in current use such as self-esteem, self-concept and motivation.

There are sound theoretical and pragmatic grounds for doubting the usefulness of global measures of motivation. H.W. Marsh (1990) has provided evidence that children's self-perception of their own ability can vary, depending on the type of task they are working on. Other studies demonstrate consistently that children's self-perceptions of ability can affect their motivational style (e.g. Nicholls, 1984; Elliott and Dweck, 1988). A useful test of any psychological theory is whether it fits everyday experience. As children or adolescents, few of us were equally confident with every subject of the school curriculum. Most of us considered ourselves successful at some and relative, or absolute, failures at others. Our perceptions of our own abilities, together with a lot of other influences such as liking a teacher and beliefs about a subject's eventual usefulness, influenced our decisions on what subjects to study for public examinations.

Motivation seems likely, then, to vary from subject to subject. It does not follow, however, that we should necessarily expect to find differences between our English and mathematics tests in the number of pupils showing adaptive or maladaptive motivational styles. If responses have a similar distribution within each of these two subjects, we will not find significant differences between them provided that the sample is large enough. It would still be useful to know more about the reasons for an individual pupil's response, but there would be no obvious evidence that one subject elicited more positive, or negative, motivational responses than the other. In contrast, if we do find differences between the two subjects, this will be prima facie evidence for the importance of the structure of the curriculum and/or of teaching methods.

This point is particularly important in view of recent discussion in Britain about the structure of the primary curriculum. The National Curriculum is organised as a number of separate subjects, and is assessed on this basis. Most primary schools, however, have retained a commitment to generalist class teachers who teach all or most of the subjects of the National Curriculum. They have also retained a commitment to organising at least part of the curriculum around a series of topics, as a way of retaining the supposedly 'seamless web' of the curriculum, thus enabling children to learn without the constraints of artificial subject boundaries. This approach has recently come under sustained attack (e.g. Alexander *et al.*, 1992; NCC, 1993; Ofsted, 1993; Alexander, 1992). Yet if the primary curriculum is to move increasingly in a more subject-specific direction, we should at least be aware of the possible implications for children's motivation. More specifically, if the primary curriculum is increasingly to be based on subjects rather than built around topics, we should know if motivational problems are more likely to be associated with some subjects than others. Our methodology only allowed us to investigate aspects of two subjects, but that is nevertheless a start.

Curriculum subject and motivational style: evidence

Methodology

We summarised our methodology in Chapter 3. At this stage we only need to comment on the construction of the English and mathematics tests. The English tests were *not* intended to be representative of the English curriculum. By focusing on comprehension of a passage of prose, we were addressing an important skill, but it quite clearly included only one aspect of the English curriculum. At the planning stage we considered the possibility of including more wide-ranging items in the English tests, but the limited time available for each of the tests made this impractical. The mathematics tests were more comprehensive, with items of arithmetic, algebra and geometry. Yet these, too, made no attempt at representative coverage of the whole curriculum. In particular we did not include any aspects of investigatory or exploratory mathematics as envisaged in Attainment Target 1 of the National Curriculum. Again, time was the deciding factor. The tests did not, therefore, allow a comparison between mathematics and English but rather a comparison between aspects of mathematics and one aspect of English.

The key questions we were investigating at this stage were:

(a) Are the maladaptive motivational styles of learned helplessness and self-worth motivation more prevalent in the responses of pupils to aspects of one of the National Curriculum core subjects of English and mathematics than to the other?

(b) In what ways are age, gender, ethnic origin and non-verbal reasoning ability related to (a) above?

(c) Are responses to the sub-scales of Nicholls' (1989) Motivational Orientation Scale influenced by the subject to which pupils are responding?

Age and motivational style in aspects of mathematics and English

Table 5.1 shows the distribution of motivational styles in English comprehension and in mathematics in each of the four year groups: Years 6, 7, 9 and 11. It also shows the percentage of pupils within each motivational style in each of the four year groups.

There are significant differences between English comprehension and mathematics in all four year groups in the number of mastery oriented children in mathematics. Children are significantly more likely to be mastery oriented in mathematics than in English comprehension irrespective of year group. In Years 6 and 11 both learned helplessness and self-worth motivation are significantly more prevalent in English comprehension than in mathematics, though in Years 7 and 9 only learned helplessness is significantly more prevalent. Overall these findings provide evidence of a higher prevalence of maladaptive motivational styles in English comprehension than in aspects of mathematics, irrespective of year group. Table 5.1 also shows a drop in mastery orientation between the final year of primary education (Year 6) and the first year of secondary education (Year 7), but we return to this in Chapter 6.

Gender and motivational style in aspects of English and mathematics

The distribution of motivational styles in each of the two subjects was similar for boys and girls and showed a higher rate of maladaptive motivational style in English comprehension than in mathematics irrespective of gender. Girls were significantly more likely to show mastery orientation in the mathematics tests than in English comprehension. Conversely, they were significantly more likely to show learned helplessness in English than in mathematics in all years except Year 6. The results for boys were similar except that Year 6 boys had a higher rate of learned helplessness in English comprehension than mathematics and Year 11 boys were significantly more likely to show a self-worth motivated response in English comprehension than in mathematics (Galloway *et al.*, 1996).

Table 5.1 *Age and motivational style in aspects of English and mathematics*

Motivational style	Year 6* Maths N=412 (%)	English N=413 (%)	LLR[†] df=1	Year 7 Maths N=320 (%)	English N=290 (%)	LLR[†] df=1	Year 9 Maths N=270 (%)	English N=269 (%)	LLR[†] df=1	Year 11 Maths N=252 (%)	English N=241 (%)	LLR[†] df=1
Mastery orientation	70.9	54.5	23.84 $p<0.001$	43.1	26.2	19.34 $p<0.001$	53.7	31.2 $p<0.001$	28.13	57.1	31.1 $p<0.001$	34.24
Learned helplessness	14.3	19.4	3.77 $p<0.05$	30.9	51.7	27.37 $p<0.001$	23.3	40.8	19.24 $p<0.001$	33.3	51.4	16.67 $p<0.001$
Self-worth motivation	14.8	26.2	16.47 $p<0.001$	25.9	22.1	1.25 NS	22.9	27.8	1.72 NS	9.5	17.4	6.70 $p<0.01$

* Year 6 figures include all data from feeder primary schools.
† Log likelihood ratio.

Ethnic origin and motivational style in aspects of English and mathematics

European and Asian pupils in each year group were both significantly more likely to be identified as mastery oriented in mathematics than in English comprehension, with the possible exception of Asian children in Year 6 for whom the difference between the two subjects was not statistically significant. White pupils were significantly more likely to be identified as learned helpless in English comprehension than in mathematics, and in Years 6 and 11 they were significantly more likely to be self-worth motivated in English comprehension. The pattern of maladaptive motivational style for Asian children was less clear, with a significant difference between subjects in the prevalence both of learned helplessness and of self-worth only in Year 7.

Non-verbal reasoning and motivational style in aspects of English and mathematics

We also analysed the distribution of motivational styles in the two subjects in each of the four non-verbal reasoning bands for children in Year 7 only. We did not have a complete set of non-verbal reasoning scores for the other year groups. There were three striking points in the results. First, we found no significant differences between the two subjects in Band 1. Hence, the evidence suggests that these very able children were able to overcome the negatively motivating aspects of the English tests, and were as likely to show mastery orientation in these as in the mathematics tests. Second, Bands 2 and 3 showed the familiar pattern of higher rate of mastery orientation in mathematics than in English comprehension, and a higher rate of learned helplessness in English comprehension than in mathematics. Third, although the tendency is in the same direction in Band 4, the difference is not quite so marked. These pupils have higher rates of maladaptive motivational style, and the evidence points towards a more globally maladaptive motivational orientation, which is less influenced by the nature of the task than in pupils in Bands 2 and 3.

Responses to Nicholls' Motivational Orientation Scale

As explained in Chapters 2 and 4, statistical analysis of Nicholls' scale identified three sub-scales: task orientation, measuring commitment to master a task or skill rather than to demonstrate competence in it; ego orientation, connoting motivation to increase a sense of self-worth by demonstrating superiority over peers; and work avoidance. Having obtained these sub-scales we were able to compare the mean score for each sub-scale on the mathematics and English comprehension versions of the scale. The results showed no important differences between the two subjects on the work avoidance sub-scale. In contrast, scores on the other two sub-scales were significantly higher in mathematics than in English comprehension using combined evidence from Years 7, 9 and 11. The differences were most marked in Years 7 and 9 for the task orientation sub-scale and in Year 7 for ego orientation. This indicates not only a stronger motivation to master a task for its own sake in mathematics, but also a stronger motivation to compete successfully with other pupils in this subject.

Comment

The consistency between the results of Nicholls' Motivational Orientation Scale and the results of curriculum-based tests is reassuring, but we still have to interpret the results. Caution is necessary here. We were not only investigating two different subjects but, arguably, also widely disparate skills. The mathematics tests contained a range of arithmetic, algebra and geometry problems which could be tackled in a short period of time. They did not include tasks requiring sustained investigation or exploration of mathematical problems. Similarly, the focus on comprehension of a passage of prose in the English tasks precluded any attention to a wide range of other skills required in the English curriculum, for example, spelling or creative writing. In other words, because the Craske technique was comparing aspects of mathematics with one aspect of English, attention should perhaps focus on the nature of the tasks rather than on the two subjects themselves. That point, however, does not apply in the same way to Nicholls' scale which asked general questions about pupils' work in English and mathematics. There is no reason to suppose that any one type of task would predominate. That said, the results indicate quite strongly that two related factors may exert a powerful influence on pupils' motivational responses. Both have attracted too little attention in motivational research.

First, the structure of a subject seems likely to influence pupils' responses when they encounter a problem. In this connection, children are likely to be more certain whether or not they have produced 'correct' answers in mathematics than in English. In other words there is often less ambiguity in mathematics. In another research project, a teacher told us that she would never mark children's work wrong in mathematics, as she felt this could lower their self-esteem. The children, though, were not fooled. They knew that the absence of a tick meant that they had not given the correct answer.

One of the attractions of mathematics lies in its clarity, with the associated possibility of obtaining a clear-cut result in a concise and elegant way. In discussing our work with some mathematics teachers, though, we have often found them surprisingly defensive about this, wishing to argue that mathematics contains opportunities for creative thinking and for exploration, drawing on very similar skills to those required in, for example, creative writing. This is not the time to debate that particular question. It is clear, however, that a large proportion of time in mathematics classes is spent on tasks similar to those in our tests. Whatever else may be said of the commitment to exploratory and investigatory work in mathematics in Attainment Target 1 of the National Curriculum, there are very few schools where this approach is the dominant influence. Our argument is simply that from the pupils' perspective there is relatively little ambiguity in mathematics compared with many other subjects.

In contrast, the scope for ambiguity in many aspects of the English curriculum is much greater. There is no correct answer in a piece of creative writing, and to a considerably lesser extent a similar point can be made about English comprehension. Some answers, certainly, will be unambiguously wrong, but it is easier for the teacher to disguise an incorrect or half-correct response by asking further questions or by making remarks such as: 'You may be on the right lines but . . .'. It could be argued that there is a parallel in mathematics when pupils demonstrate understanding of a problem without making accurate calculations; nevertheless, pupils will still be aware that the end product is not entirely acceptable.

The amount of ambiguity in the structure of a subject has implications for pupils' motivation in tackling difficult tasks. We need not waste time on the discredited sentimentality implicit in the view that children should never be given tasks on which they might fail. If the concept of achieving their full potential means anything, it implies a gap between level of attainment and level of aspiration – whether the latter is based on the teacher's goals or the pupil's. In turn, this implies the possibility of not succeeding on a task which aims to bridge that gap. Our point is that children's motivation to persevere is likely to be stronger when they understand, or at least think they understand, what they have to do to overcome the problem – in other words, when the ambiguity in the task is reduced.

If mastery orientation is the goal, the problem of ambiguity in the task is compounded by that of feedback from the teacher. As we argued earlier, the teacher who refused to mark mathematics work incorrect could not mislead the children. English teachers, in contrast, can give much more ambiguous feedback under the guise of encouraging children to keep trying: 'You're on the right lines but . . .', or 'A good try and . . .'. Such responses may actually be counter-productive if they leave children uncertain that their initial response was unacceptable, *and* feeling that their teacher is quite satisfied with their efforts so far. Thus, ambiguity in the subject may be associated with ambiguity in feedback. The problem is that it is precisely when unambiguous feedback is needed for motivational purposes that it is least likely to be offered. This does, however, suggest that teachers may play a crucial role in fostering an adaptive motivational style, and we must now consider the importance not only of teachers as individuals, but also of the school as a social institution.

Motivational style, and school and teacher effectiveness

Since the seminal reports on secondary school effectiveness by Rutter *et al.* (1979) and on primary school effectiveness by Mortimore *et al.* (1988), interest in the school's contribution to pupils' progress and adjustment has continued at a high level. Mortimore's work is of particular interest here in showing the influence of school climate on children's self-concept. Although a majority of studies have focused on pupils' educational progress, it is also clear that schools exert a very powerful effect on non-cognitive outcomes, such as pupils' behaviour.

Galloway (1995) has argued that factors within the school are the dominant influences on pupils' behaviour in the school, and are of greater importance than factors in the home background. He has also cited substantial evidence that school factors are critical in determining the number of exclusions from school, though these are not the same factors that affect behaviour in the classroom. In contrast, social factors in the home background are of greater importance in truancy and delinquency, though the school still has an important influence: both problems increase in prevalence throughout the secondary school years, and both correlate quite highly with measures of social disadvantage. The position with educational progress is slightly more complicated. Obviously, it is unrealistic to evaluate schools against specific outcomes, for example, GCSE results, if there are wide variations between schools in the attainments of pupils on admission. (Although we say that this point is 'obvious', it seems to have escaped Her Majesty's Inspectors of Schools, and for many years HMI and Ofsted reports have continued to compare results against the national average.)

With the introduction of league tables, attention has focused on the school's 'value added' contribution, i.e. the amount of progress which is due to the school, as opposed to the progress which can be expected as a result of the normal process of maturation. There is general agreement, though, that although the differences in effectiveness between schools are educationally and socially important, the differences between teachers are greater than the differences between schools (e.g. Mortimore *et al.*, 1988). In other words, we might expect to find a wider variation in effectiveness between teachers within the same school than we might find between schools. The implication here is clear: while the quality of leadership and other organisational factors are critically important, the classroom teacher also plays a crucial part in determining the quality of pupils' learning experiences in school. Given the importance of motivation, it has been surprisingly neglected in school and teacher effectiveness research. While conventional staffroom wisdom might see high motivation as an indication of school and teacher effectiveness, none of the major studies have investigated systematically the possibility of variation between schools and between teachers in the motivational responses they elicit from their pupils.

Differences between schools

We started by placing the data from curriculum testing in each of the primary schools in rank order of the percentage of pupils in each motivational style. Table 5.2 shows the data for English Comprehension. The percentage of mastery-oriented children ranges from 71 per cent (Schools 4 and 2) to 42 per cent (Schools 7 and 10). In the case of learned helplessness the range is, if anything, even more striking, from 39 per cent of all pupils (School 10) to a mere 4 per cent (School 2). Overall, these differences were statistically significant, with Schools 8 and 10 standing out as having an exceptionally high rate of learned helplessness, School 2 an exceptionally low rate of learned helplessness and School 7 an exceptionally high rate of self-worth motivation. The results for mathematics were broadly similar, but less marked.

We also investigated the relationship between motivational style on the curriculum-based tests and the mean scores on sub-scales from Nicholls' Motivational Orientation Scale. Again, the results were clearer for English than for mathematics and four schools stood out. When we combined both sets of results.

School 2:   low in learned helplessness and high on work avoidance sub-scale.

School 7:   high in self-worth motivation and high on work avoidance sub-scale.

Schools 8 and 10: high in learned helplessness and low in ego involvement sub-scales.

These results merit further discussion. School 2 had a high rate of mastery orientation; the low rate of learned helplessness might therefore

Table 5.2 English: rank order of schools by percentage of pupils in each motivational style (excluding uncategorised)

School code	Mastery %	School code	Self-worth %	School code	Learned helplessness %
4	71.4	7	50.0	10	39.2
2	71.1	6	42.3	8	34.7
1	57.9	1	34.2	9	26.7
11	56.6	3	30.3	11	22.6
3	51.5	2	22.4	3	18.2
9	48.9	9	24.4	6	15.4
8	42.9	4	23.8	7	8.3
6	42.3	8	22.4	1	7.9
7	41.7	11	20.8	4	4.8
10	41.7	10	13.7	2	4.4

* School 5 dropped from this analysis because of insufficient numbers.

Note:

$df = 18$

Log likelihood ratio (LLR) = 52.41

$p < 0.000$

be predicted, but the high mean rating on the work avoidance sub-scale suggests that mastery orientation can be accompanied by motivation to complete the task with the minimum of effort. Conversely, the combination in School 7 of a high rate of self-worth motivation with a high rating on work avoidance suggests that pupils in this school tended to use conscious avoidance of work as a way of protecting themselves from the risk of failure. The evidence from Schools 8 and 10 is less surprising. For these pupils, learned helplessness tended to coincide with relatively low motivation for competition with other pupils.

Turning to the secondary schools, we initially combined data for Years 7, 9 and 11 in each subject (Table 5.3). In English the rate of mastery orientation was significantly higher at Summertown, the school with a high rate of social disadvantage, than at Springtown which served an affluent suburban area. The rate of learned helplessness was almost identical at the two schools, but Springtown had more self-worth motivated pupils. In mathematics this picture was reversed. Mastery orientation was significantly higher at Springtown, self-worth motivation at Summertown, with each school having almost the same percentage of learned helpless pupils. In other words there was something about the English Department at Summertown and the mathematics Department at Springtown which encouraged mastery orientation. This is consistent with other evidence which shows that differences between subject departments in a school are greater than differences between schools. It also shows that although mastery orientation was more common in mathematics than in English in both schools, the extent of the difference could be affected by the quality of teaching, or at least by Departmental organisation.

The GCSE results at Springtown School were substantially better than at Summertown, as defined by the overall pass rate and grades. Yet Summertown had the higher rate of mastery orientation. At first sight this is disconcerting. Theoretically, we should expect mastery oriented pupils to do better. This brings us back to the question of 'value added', or the proportion of pupils' achievements which are attributable to the school as opposed to the effects of maturation. Ideally, we would have investigated this by using attainment scores at age 11 as a way of predicting GCSE grade at age 16. We would then have been able to examine whether pupils in one of the two schools achieved higher, or lower, GCSE grades than had been predicted. This *might* have shown that Summertown pupils had indeed done better than Springtown pupils. On the other hand, it might have shown the reverse. However, we had no information about the attainments of Year 11 pupils when they entered secondary school.

Table 5.3 Motivational style in two secondary schools: Years 7, 9 and 11 combined

	English			Mathematics		
	Springtown N=364 (%)	Summertown N=436 (%)	LLR	Springtown N=395 (%)	Summertown N=447 (%)	LLR
Mastery orientation	25.5	32.6	4.74 $p<0.05$	54.4	47.4	4.12 $p<0.05$
Learned helplessness	48.4	47.7	0.03 NS	29.1	29.3	0.0003 NS
Self-worth motivation	26.1	19.7	4.59 $p<0.05$	16.5	23.3	6.12 $p<0.02$

Differences between teachers

Few of the primary schools had more than one teacher with a Year 6 class, and comparison between teachers was therefore unlikely to add much to the comparisons between schools. In the secondary schools, though, we were able to compare the motivational styles of pupils taught by different teachers. We excluded teachers with fewer than 20 pupils; these teachers normally had very small classes of pupils with Statements of special educational needs. We combined data for pupils in different classes taught by the same teacher. In Springtown School we found significant differences between English teachers in the number of mastery oriented pupils, but not between mathematics teachers, with a range from 12 per cent to 36 per cent. There were no significant differences in either subject between teachers in the number of pupils with a maladaptive motivational style. In Summertown School, too, we found significant differences between English teachers in the number of mastery oriented pupils, and in this school the same was true of mathematics teachers, with a range from 38 per cent to 70 per cent.

Comment and conclusions

These results illustrate the complexity of the concept of motivation. Thus, the exceptionally high rates of mastery orientation *and* of work avoidance in schools can be understood in terms of a high motivation to complete tasks with the minimum effort, but that interpretation merely underlines the importance of a more detailed understanding of teaching and learning processes within each school. What the results do confirm quite unequivocally is the impact of schools, departments within secondary schools, and teachers on pupils' motivation. The results from the English and mathematics departments at the two secondary schools are particularly interesting. Summertown was significantly higher than Springtown in mastery orientation in English, but Springtown significantly higher in mathematics. In each case the school with the lower rate of mastery orientation had a significantly higher rate of self-worth motivation, suggesting that pupils protected themselves against the threat of failure by devaluing the importance of the subject. Given the huge differences between the two schools in their pupil intake, we cannot draw firm conclusions from the higher rate of mastery orientation at Summertown, but the results do indicate the need for caution before assuming any direct relationship between motivational style and educational progress. Pupils who opt out of challenging tasks may be increasing their chances of success in relatively undemanding tasks.

Taken together, the results in Chapter 4 and in this chapter have demonstrated the influence of individual differences, curriculum subject, and school factors on pupils' motivational style. These influences were more striking than those of gender or race, though the influence of the former was by no means negligible. The increased tendency of pupils with low non-verbal reasoning and low educational attainment to demonstrate maladaptive motivational style was noteworthy, but a more consistent and less predictable finding was the heightened tendency towards a maladaptive style following a difficult task in English comprehension compared with mathematics.

We now need to turn to the impact of transfer to secondary school. This does not just involve a change of school. It also involves a change in teaching methods, in curriculum organisation, in parents' expectations and, possibly, in teachers' expectations; and all these changes coincide with the physical changes of puberty. The motivational implications are potentially enormous, and are discussed in Chapter 6.

CHAPTER SIX

Transfer from primary to secondary school and changes in the secondary school years

Introduction

We have demonstrated a relationship between maladaptive motivational style and special educational need at least until the later years of secondary education. More interestingly, perhaps we have also shown that the English and mathematics tasks which we gave pupils in Years 6, 7, 9 and 11 elicited substantially different motivational responses. The comparisons between schools and teachers were less clear-cut but nevertheless consistent with the view that pupils' motivational style is powerfully influenced, for better or worse, by the situation in which they find themselves. This chapter is concerned with two potentially important influences on motivation which we have not so far addressed. The first is the effect of transfer to secondary school, which for pupils in our sample took place at the beginning of Year 7 (age 11–12). The second is the effect of greater maturity as pupils progress from their first year in secondary school to the final year of compulsory schooling (in Britain, Year 11, or age 15–16).

Primary–secondary transfer involves not only a change of school, but also a structural change. Almost invariably, children find themselves in a larger school with a more clearly subject-based curriculum and a different teacher for each subject. The impact of this structural change in the context of schooling coincides with the onset of puberty and adolescence. Distinguishing between the effect of these two potential influences on motivational style is probably impossible, but we should at least be able to show whether any significant change take place between Years 6 and 7 and subsequent to Year 7.

It was impractical to follow the same group of pupils beyond Years 6–7 as the fieldwork for our project had to be completed within two years. Thus, although we followed a group of children from their final year in primary school to their first year in secondary, we had to select two different 'cross-sectional' samples of pupils in Years 9 and 11 (see

Chapter 3). This chapter will review the evidence from other sources about changes in motivational style between the ages of 10–11 and 11–12. We shall also discuss possible mechanisms and underlying processes which may be responsible for the changes which have been reported. We shall then turn to the results of our own project. First, we shall show that for many pupils secondary school transfer was associated with a significant increase in maladaptive motivational style. Next we shall show that although an increase in mastery orientation has occurred by Years 9 and 11, this does not reach the level of the final year of primary education, and the general picture masks important differences between groups of pupils.

Motivational style following transfer to secondary school

The views of primary heads

After securing the co-operation of two comprehensive secondary schools, our next task was to seek that of 11 of the feeder primary schools. This required extensive – and stimulating – discussion with the headteachers concerned. The project depended on them agreeing to take part and it was therefore with considerable relief that we discovered that most of the primary heads, while naturally being concerned with the practicalities of involvement with the project – the amount of time it would take and so on – were nevertheless keenly interested in the problem of motivation over the transfer from primary to secondary school.

The common element in the headteachers' view was that the transfer from Year 6 to Year 7 proved to be anti-climactic and therefore demotivating for their ex-pupils. There were two reasons for this. First, the pupils had been looking forward, with eager anticipation, to moving into the world of secondary school. Other small-scale studies by primary headteachers (e.g. Burke, 1993) illustrate similar concerns that positive forms of motivation can be difficult to maintain during the later stages of Year 6 as pupils increasingly come to see themselves as being essentially detached from primary school and as secondary school pupils in waiting.

Second, however, the primary school heads also expressed the view that the actual experience of secondary schooling during Year 7, was disappointing. They attributed this disappointment to the lack of intellectual demands made of the pupils by the Year 7 teachers. One of our primary school heads summed up this view when he told us about a meeting with his ex-pupils towards the end of their Year 7; when he asked them what they had been doing, the answer generally was 'very little'. This lack of demand led to a perceived reduction in the extent to which school could be seen as challenging and therefore a corresponding decrease in their motivation for schoolwork.

These ideas reflect the views about the experience of motivation developed by Csikszentmihalyi (1992) and his colleagues in which optimal motivational states are formed when individuals perceive themselves to be highly competent in an area of activity in which they are currently being highly challenged. Tasks that are too demanding produce anxiety which can inhibit performance (e.g. Willig *et al.*, 1987; Covington, 1992) and ultimately helplessness. Tasks that present demands too much below a person's self-perceived level of competence produce disinterest, apathy and boredom.

The primary school headteachers' view, then, was that transfer to secondary school does cause motivational problems. These problems are to do with limitations in the organisation of the curriculum leading to an intellectually unstimulating Year 7 environment for many pupils, particularly the brighter ones. Our fieldwork took place in the relatively early stages of the implementation of the National Curriculum. It is not surprising, therefore, that these primary school headteachers looked to the National Curriculum itself as a possible solution to these problems. In time, they suggested, the National Curriculum ought to provide a single framework within which both primary and secondary schools would be operating, thereby providing a seamless transfer from Year 6 to Year 7 for pupils across the ability range. One further point that can be made here is that quite clearly implicit in the headteachers' views, and stated explicitly by some, the difficult to teach were not only to be found among the less able; the more able pupil in some ways provided the greater challenge to those concerned with the management of the curriculum over the middle years of schooling.

Potential motivational problems in primary–secondary transfer

Before turning to other research we need to ask why transfer may be problematic. The two principal maladaptive motivational styles identified in Chapter 2 were, of course, self-worth motivation and learned helplessness. A common thread running through conceptions of these two styles involves pupils' perceptions of their own levels of ability and their conception of ability itself, in particular whether they see ability as something fixed and static, or something which can be developed.

For Covington (1992) the self-worth motive is associated with views of the cultural significance attached to high levels of ability and anxieties which follow from threats, or anticipated threats, to that conception of the self as competent. The transfer to secondary school from primary school is clearly likely to be an anxious time for many pupils for a number of reasons. Not all of these will be related to a sense of academic ability and therefore relevant to a sense of academic self-worth, but the transition to a new set of curriculum-related demands undeniably carries with it the potential for children to become anxious about their level of ability. Interestingly, the anticipation of such threats to children's sense of self-worth might be more anxiety provoking than the reality of the curriculum tasks which they actually experience on arrival at secondary school.

The transfer to secondary school may also be associated with increases in learned helplessness if increasing numbers of pupils come to see themselves as being unable to meet the curriculum demands made of them, and as being unable to do anything about improving this situation. Again it is the student's perception of their abilities and of the demands of the tasks presented to them that will be critical (Dweck, 1985).

Reasons for expecting motivational change

As explained in Chapter 2, the background to our study lies in work carried out in the USA and it is naturally the case that most of the more immediately relevant empirical data relating to the motivational effects of transfer comes from the same source. A detailed reading of this work shows many similarities between the USA and England in terms of the nature of the changes involved when a child transfers from primary to secondary, or elementary to middle or junior high school. As indicated in the review by Eccles *et al.* (1984), the secondary school will usually be larger, will group classes by ability or attainment, and whole-class teaching by subject specialist teachers will be more common. The general ethos will be more competitive and focused on ability rather than effort. Perhaps more surprisingly, as shown by Brophy and Evertson (1978), the transfer between schools is also associated with an increase in the amount of teacher control that is evident within the classroom. Brophy and Evertson's work suggests that this increase in teacher control stems from the increase in subject specialist teaching which, in turn, reduces total weekly contact between any one teacher and their pupils, and from the growth of identification with peers rather than with adults, including teachers, during the period of adolescence. The growth of identification with peers can, of course, be a positive motivational influence, for example, when high-achieving pupils compete with each other, but it can also be a negative influence, as when a group of pupils become convinced that they cannot achieve success on the terms set by the school.

Brophy and Evertson's work indicates the probable importance of a change in the structure of schooling and of a developmental change in young people themselves. While Brophy and Evertson focused on identification with a peer group, however, Nicholls (1989) sharpened the focus of motivational research upon the concept of ability, or rather the concepts of ability held by children. In a series of studies, Nicholls gathered data which supported the view that concepts of ability, and related concepts such as those of effort and task difficulty, underlie important and motivationally significant developmental change.

In essence the process may be seen as follows. The young child operates with a view that does not make clear cause and effect distinctions and which is also egocentric in that it makes little reference to other people. Success, relatively high ability and the exertion of effort are all positive characteristics which would be expected to cluster within the same person, as would failure, relatively low ability and laziness. A similar tendency to assume a congruence of all positive or all negative characteristics in others can be seen in research that has examined the young child's perceptions of other people (Livesley and Bromley, 1973; Rogers, 1978; Zebrowitz, 1990). If high ability and success are seen to coexist this does not necessarily mean that cause and effect relationships are also assumed. In contrast to this developmental perspective, Rogers (1982) has argued, with respect to the development of more general person perception, for a functional approach. This argument essentially states that developmental change will be produced, at least in part, by changes in the demands made upon the child. As the child moves into more complex social situations, so he or she needs increasingly complex and sophisticated concepts about other people in order to make adequate interpretations of and predictions about human behaviour.

The application of a similar functional approach to the development of concepts of success and failure would focus attention on the child's understanding of that which has to be explained, namely success and failure itself. Nicholls' own research illustrates this point by describing changes in the child's understanding of 'difficulty'. For the younger child, still in the early primary school years, the notion of difficulty is entirely egocentric. Those tasks which the child cannot accomplish are difficult, those which can be done are easy. By the end of primary schooling this has given way to a more clearly normative definition of difficulty. A difficult task is now one which most people cannot achieve, an easy task is one which most people can. There is an immediate and most important consequence of this change. When the normative definition is in operation a child's own performance can be independent of the difficulty of the task – it is possible to succeed on tasks that are difficult and fail on those that are normatively easy. This, logically, could not be the case at the earlier egocentric stage. The development of the normative understanding of difficulty creates for the child, then, further problems or puzzles which need solving. In the process of solving them children come to develop further their understandings of ability and effort.

This later development involves the making of two clear distinctions. The first is between cause and effect. Effort, ability and related concepts come to be seen as causes of differing degrees of success and failure. Second, effort and ability become increasingly distinguishable as children get older. Effort is variable (sometimes in a controllable way, sometimes not) while ability is more likely to be seen as fixed and relatively stable. Most important, perhaps, ability comes to be seen as a capacity, an aspect of an individual that ultimately sets a limit to what one can achieve. It is this *entity* view of the nature of ability that lies behind Covington's (1992) theory of self-worth motivation and Dweck's (1985) view of learned helplessness.

The developmental point is relevant in understanding possible changes at the stage of primary–secondary transfer. In terms of Nicholls' analysis, older children, those at the end of primary schooling and at the commencement of secondary, are more likely to be operating with an entity view of ability and therefore to be at greater risk of learned helplessness and more prone to maladaptive processes discussed by Covington as part of the self-worth motive. It is possible, then, that an increase in maladaptive motivational tendencies at around the age of school transfer is likely to be a developmental effect rather than one that is related to the transfer itself.

Evidence from other research

Eccles and Midgeley (1989) have reviewed evidence from a wide range of sources that transfer from one phase of schooling to the next can be highly significant. For example, Simmons *et al.* (1973) found more detrimental effects on a number of measures of self-esteem related to academic and school concerns among 12-year-olds who had made the transition to secondary-level schooling than was the case for those of the same age who had not. However, given the difficulties generally encountered in finding consistent measures of self-esteem variables it is not surprising to find that other studies (e.g. Harter *et al.*, 1987) find declines in self-esteem irrespective of transfer, while yet others (e.g. Eccles *et al.*, 1988) find no age- or transfer-related changes.

In relation to measures of anxiety – an important component of the self-worth motive, Harter *et al.* (1987) found that school transition rather than age itself was associated with an increase in school-related anxiety levels. However it is in relation to measures of motivational orientation itself that the effects of school transfer seem to be clearest. Following transfer, students are generally less intrinsically motivated and more extrinsically motivated, have lower levels of achievement motivation and are apparently less clear about the causes of their successes and failures. The last finding is highlighted in Eccles and Midgeley's (1989) review and is drawn from research by Connell (1980) and by Connell and Tero (1982). As will be seen later, this finding suggests that some of the negative impact of transfer may be relatively short-lived. For example, if an initial confusion about the causes of success and failure under a new regime gives rise to feelings of relative powerlessness and a lack of personal control (thus leading to increases in maladaptive motivational responses) it is not unreasonable to suggest that as students become familiar with the new regime and develop ways and means of understanding it, so feelings of personal control will increase and motivation improve. It is important, then, to distinguish between the effects of transfer as such and the effects of being in secondary rather than primary school.

A further point to note here is the potential mismatch between the growing wishes, and indeed needs, of the adolescent for greater autonomy and the greater degree of control which teachers may exert over young people at this stage in their education and development (Eccles and Midgeley, 1989; Brophy and Evertson, 1978). Increasing homework and examination pressures are two obvious examples. It is not clear, though, whether a decline in adaptive motivational style at or around the time of transfer, with a corresponding increase in anxiety, is maintained throughout the period of secondary schooling.

Finally, there is one further aspect of the findings of previous research which needs to be attended to. Although the results of many studies show a general decline in measures of motivation and self-esteem associated with school transition and with individual development, it is important to note variations across this theme. For example, Eccles *et al.* (1987) report a decline in attitudes towards mathematics but not towards English; similar findings from Wigfield (1984) and Eccles *et al.* (1988) also suggested that self-confidence in and attitudes towards mathematics might be more vulnerable to transitional and age-related change than was the case in English. Gotfried (1981) reported a decline for reading, mathematics, science and social studies with the greatest decline in reading and science; Prawat *et al.* (1979) showed a decline in their measures of achievement motivation during the middle years of schooling suggesting that these might be differences between the long- and short-term effects of school transition. The nature of the schools involved in the transfer are also likely to affect the outcome. Youngman (1978) studied primary to secondary transfer in England and reported variations in the degree of decline in self-concept and attitudes to school depending on the location of the school (e.g. rural or urban) and the initial characteristics of the child (e.g. those with initially lower self-concepts were more at risk to the generally negative effects of transfer than were children who undertook the transfer with a more positive self-image).

While reviews by Eccles *et al.* (1984) and Eccles and Midgeley (1989) can point with confidence to substantial evidence for a general decline in measures of achievement motivation, self-concept and a range of attitudes towards school and schoolwork, it is not possible to be at all precise about the exact causes of the changes and the causes of the variations in the degree of magnitude involved. It is clear that the generally negative effects result from a combination of both age-related development and the effects of transition. There is also some evidence to suggest that transition at around the age of 11 years may be particularly difficult (Warburton *et al.*, 1983) and that school organisation will affect the degree of change (Power, 1981). Any effects observed below from our own data need to be evaluated carefully. There will inevitably be doubts about what may properly be inferred.

Transfer and beyond

We used a variety of measures to follow pupils from Year 6, the final year of their primary schooling, into Year 7, the first year of secondary, with some additional measures taken in Year 8. In addition we had information about separate groups of pupils in Years 9 and 11.

The central technique employed in this study for identifying motivational style was the technique originally developed by Craske (1988) which enables us to determine the proportion of children demonstrating mastery orientation, learned helplessness and the self-worth motive in tasks taken from both English and mathematics.

Motivational style in four age groups

Figure 6.1 shows that the transition from Years 6 to 7 (primary to secondary school) is associated with notable drops in the percentage of pupils demonstrating mastery orientation in both English and Mathematics. The mathematics tasks show a consistently higher level of mastery orientation than those in English (see Chapter 5), but there is no evidence of a differential effect between the two subjects of the transfer itself. It is important to note that in Years 9 and 11, again to an equal degree for each subject, there is a recovery in the percentage of pupils demonstrating mastery orientation. The comparison between Years 7, 9 and 11 relate to different groups of pupils and it is necessary to be cautious in claiming that these changes are related to the effects of changes in school year rather than changes in cohort. However, the

Figure 6.1 **Percentage of pupils classified as mastery oriented in English and mathematics**

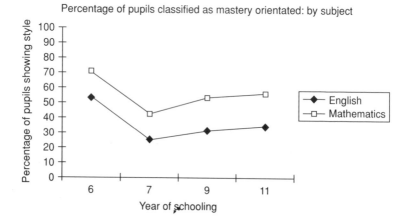

broad pattern is one that is consistent with some of the findings discussed above (e.g. Prawat *et al.*, 1979).

The drop in mastery orientation between Years 6 and 7 was matched by an increase in maladaptive motivational style, followed by a gradual reduction over the later years of secondary schooling. Year 7 showed the highest level of maladaptive motivation style, but the reduction through to Year 11 was not sufficient to restore the position obtaining in Year 6.

There was a relative increase in learned helplessness and a relative decrease in the self-worth motive between Years 9 and 11. This was in keeping with our understanding of the dynamics of these two motivational styles. Learned helpless students are ones who have come to assume that they are incapable of current success and have little or no chance of being more successful in the future. There are at least two broad ways in which this could be accounted for. One is in terms of the cumulative effect of information processing. As pupils increase their experience of schooling, so they are increasingly likely to look back over a longer history of success and failure. Those who see an accumulation of relative failure in a given area of activity are more likely to begin to attribute this to a lack of ability. The stability and uncontrollability of this cause gives rise to low expectations for future change and hence helplessness. In support of this is the finding discussed in Chapter 4 that learned helplessness is significantly more prevalent in pupils of below average ability and attainment.

It is difficult, however, to apply the same argument to an interpretation of the findings here concerning the decrease in the self-worth motive.

A better explanation, which can account for both sets of findings within a common framework, is couched in terms of goals. The dynamics of the self-worth motive assume that:

(a) academic (school-related) ability is culturally valued; and
(b) instances of relative failure threaten a positive self-concept of academic ability and that therefore
(c) defensive strategies are needed.

Of course, if (a) does not apply, neither will (b) and (c). It is possible that both the decrease in the proportion of pupils showing the self-worth motive and the increase showing learned helplessness in Year 11 (in comparison to Year 9) reflect an increase in the proportion of pupils who no longer place a significant value on academic success. In terms of the Craske procedure this would have two effects. First, an increasing number of pupils, on having Test D introduced as difficult, will simply not wish to make the effort they believe will be necessary. The value of success would not be worth the cost of the work involved. In terms of the patterns produced by the Craske procedure this is the same as their assuming that they lack the necessary ability and can do nothing about it (the 'true' learned helpless response), but in terms of process it is different. Second, a similar reduction in the value of academic success removes or reduces anxieties associated with relative academic failure and therefore reduces the proportion of pupils demonstrating the self-worth motive.

Before moving on from this section of the available data it is important to remind ourselves that over the primary–secondary transition some pupils changed from demonstrating a maladaptive style in the tests administered in Year 6, to demonstrating an adaptive, mastery oriented one in Year 7. Even in English where the overall pattern was more negative it was still the case that 24 per cent of those showing learned helplessness in Year 6, and 29 per cent of those demonstrating the self-worth motive changed to a mastery-oriented style in Year 7. Whatever the details of the processes involved in determining motivational consequences of school transition it is clear that these will have positive effects in some cases, against a generally negative background.

Perceptions of the classroom environment:
1: Class climate and pupil autonomy and control

Eccles *et al.* (1984) and Eccles and Midgeley (1989) noted a number of changes in the children's perception of the school and classroom environment following transfer. Certainly it would be odd if the overall increase in a maladaptive style were not reflected in changes in pupils' perceptions of the school or classroom. We addressed this aspect of the process of transfer with De Charms' (1976) 'origin-pawn' scale. This scale measures the degree to which pupils perceive their class as facilitating personal control over their learning. Pupils respond to each item on a 5-point scale. De Charms describes classes which are seen as operating in ways which diminish pupil autonomy and facilitate teacher control as 'pawn-like'. In contrast, 'origin-like' classes offer pupils more control over their own learning processes and are assumed to enhance motivation to learn. In Year 7, all pupils completed three versions of the origin-pawn scale. The first related to their perception of their present English class, the second to their present mathematics class and a third retrospective version to their last class in primary school. In Year 8 they completed two versions only, covering their current English and mathematics classes.

The retrospective version of the scale may not provide a valid picture of how pupils actually felt while in their final year at primary school. There is the obvious possibility that it may offer a rose-tinted view. Nevertheless, it does indicate the contrast, as seen by children in their first year at secondary school, between their present situation and their final year at primary school.

We started by using the statistical technique of principal components analysis to identify 'factors', or groups of items which children had answered in a similar way. Unlike De Charms, who found seven factors, we found four. Two identified different forms of perceived teacher control: co-operative control and emotional control; a third factor was concerned with pupil autonomy and the fourth with academic self-confidence.

We were then able to compare responses of Year 7 pupils with their retrospective perception of primary school (Year 6), and also responses provided by the same pupils in Years 7 and 8. In each case comparisons were based on the mean ratings of the items in each factor, and in the case of Years 7 and 8 for English and mathematics. Table 6.1 shows that there were no significant differences between Years 7 and 8. In contrast, the Year 7 ratings were significantly lower than the retrospective ratings on the co-operative climate and pupil autonomy sub-scales, both for English and for mathematics. In addition the self-confidence sub-scale showed a significant difference between Year 7 and the retrospective measure in mathematics, though not in English.

These findings are largely consistent with those reviewed at the beginning of this chapter. As they look back to their last year in primary school in contrast to their current situation, pupils see a primary classroom in which they had a teacher who allowed them to help each other more, who liked them and who they could approach for help (co-operative climate);

Table 6.1 **Mean scores on sub-scales of De Charms' origin-pawn scale for longitudinal sample in Years 7 and 8**

	1 Year 6 Retrospective measure	2 Year 7 English	3 Year 7 Maths	4 Year 8 English	5 Year 8 Maths	Statistical significance (Paired *t* test)	
						Years 6–7	Years 7–8
Co-operative climate	3.93	3.31	3.43	3.22	3.43	1 & 2 $p<0.01$ 1 & 3 $p<0.01$	NS
Emotional control	3.75	3.69	3.78	3.81	3.65	NS	NS
Pupil autonomy	3.00	2.19	2.37	2.16	2.26	1 & 2 $p<0.01$ 1 & 3 $p<0.01$	NS
Self-confidence	4.01	3.91	3.88	3.93	3.88	1 & 3 $p<0.04$	NS

Note: Number of pupils varies between 197–217.

a classroom in which they had greater autonomy in determining how to go about their work and use their time; and where they had greater self-confidence than they do in secondary mathematics classes. The degree to which the teacher exercised emotional control through getting angry and upset remains the same.

The finding that self-confidence appears relatively low in mathematics is in keeping with studies reviewed earlier (e.g. Eccles *et al.*, 1983, 1984). This reported decline in self-concept measures relates to mathematics but not English over the period of the school transition. This seems in contrast with our findings relating to motivational style which generally show greater motivational problems in English than in mathematics.

Perceptions of the classroom environment: 2: Task and ego orientation

Nicholls' (1989) Motivational Orientation Scale offered us a further means of evaluating the transfer to secondary school from the pupils' perspective. The results we obtained were consistent with those of Nicholls (1989) in USA. Statistical analysis identified three sub-scales. These enabled us to observe changes in motivation to master a task for its own sake ('task orientation'), to increase a sense of self-worth by demonstrating superiority over peers ('ego orientation') and to avoid work ('work avoidance').

Children in the longitudinal sample completed the scale in Year 6 and again in Year 7. We were therefore able to calculate the mean score for each sub-scale in each age group. Table 6.2 shows a significant increase in Year 7 over Year 6 on scores in all three sub-scales in mathematics, and on the ego orientation sub-scale in English.

In both subjects, as would be predicted from the existing literature, there is an increase in ego orientation from Year 6 to Year 7. In Year 7 pupils are more likely to express concern with developing and protecting their own sense of self-worth than they are in Year 6. In addition to this pupils express more concern with avoiding work in mathematics: feeling good about school seems to be increasingly associated with getting away with doing as little as possible. However, there is also a significant increase in task orientation in mathematics that is not found in English, although the trend is in the same direction.

Relationship between measures

The pattern of change observed with both the De Charms measure and the Nicholls sub-scales is consistent with the findings from the Craske

Table 6.2 Mean scores on sub-scales of Nicholls' Motivational Orientation Scale: longitudinal sample

	Year 6 English	Year 7 English	Statistical significance	Year 6 Mathematics	Year 7 Mathematics	Statistical significance
Task orientation	2.05	2.12	NS	2.01	2.11	$p<0.01$
Ego orientation	2.51	2.90	$p<0.001$	2.45	2.90	$p<0.001$
Work avoidance	2.77	2.92	NS	2.71	2.92	$p<0.02$

Note: Number of pupils varies between 208–217.

procedure. The Craske results show an increase in maladaptive and a decrease in adaptive styles following transfer from primary to secondary school. De Charms' scale shows how pupils themselves saw the primary school as a more autonomous environment which generally encouraged a more positively motivating approach to learning. This retrospectively positive view of the primary school is what one would expect to find in a group of pupils who have typically lost positive forms of motivation over the transfer.

With the Nicholls sub-scales a more complex picture emerges as there is evidence of both positive and negative change from a motivational perspective. Both ego orientation and work avoidance increase, the latter only in mathematics. However, again for mathematics only, there is a positive increase in task orientation.

At this stage, though, an important *caveat* is necessary. We cannot assume that the three scales are all measuring the same thing – and indeed if they were, there would be no point in using more than one. While they all show the negative effect of transfer, with some qualification in the case of Nicholls' scale, it does not follow that the children with maladaptive motivational styles on Craske's technique are those who have low mean scores on Nicholls' task orientation sub-scale or the highest sub-scale scores on De Charms' instrument.

We examined the relationship between motivational style as assessed by Craske's technique and children's sense of personal control over their environment as assessed on De Charms' scale. To do so, we calculated the difference between the mean scores for Year 7 and the Year 6 retrospective measure on each of De Charms' sub-scales. Both for English and mathematics, Year 7 pupils tended to see their last primary class in a more favourable light. However, these difference scores show a good deal of variability. So while the average child, for example, saw her or his ex-primary classroom as allowing more personal autonomy than the current mathematics classroom, there were many pupils for whom the opposite was the case.

Conclusions

The consistent picture to emerge from work on transfer to secondary school is that it is associated with a decline in adaptive forms of motivation. Overall, the evidence from De Charms' scale suggests that this is associated more strongly with the pupils' response to the change in school and curriculum organisation than with developmental changes associated with adolescence. If the latter were of paramount importance, we would have expected to find significant gender differences at the time of transfer, as the onset of puberty is typically earlier in girls than in boys. We did not, however, find evidence for this (see Chapter 4). Evidence from pupils aged 13–14 (Year 9) and 15–16 (Year 11) indicates an increase in mastery orientation by comparison with 11- to 12-year-olds (Year 7) but not to the same level as children in their last year at primary school.

The overall trend from our three motivation measures is clear. Motivation declines over the primary–secondary transfer. However, there is sufficient variation in some of the detail revealed within each measure to suggest that these are each examining different aspects of the motivational process, and that each aspect might be influenced somewhat differently by the changes found in secondary school. It is also important not to lose sight of the fact that, on each of the instruments, not every child shows a decline in motivation over the transfer. In other words, the transfer from primary to secondary school can have different effects depending on the circumstances of the transfer. Changes in the curriculum, teachers and teaching methods interact with more general aspects of school organisation to influence children's motivation. The overriding message remains the same: motivational style can be and is influenced by changes in the child's experience. Before examining the implications for schools and teachers in Part 3, we need to look in more detail at how some of the children in our sample made sense, in motivational terms, of their experience of the tests in the Craske instrument.

CHAPTER SEVEN

Children's perspectives on motivation

Introduction

The evidence from the work we have described so far suggests that neither gender nor ethnicity exert a major influence on motivational style in the ways we have investigated it. There is evidence that children with special educational needs are more likely to show a maladaptive motivational style than others. In keeping with the Warnock Report (DES, 1978) and current legislation we adopted a wide-ranging definition of special educational needs, to include a large minority of pupils in ordinary schools. The evidence seems consistent with the conventional wisdom in most staffrooms that pupils with special educational needs have problems of low self-esteem and poor motivation. In contrast, the much stronger and more consistent evidence that maladaptive motivational styles are more prevalent in English comprehension than in aspects of mathematics would probably cause more surprise. In addition, given the amount of time and effort spent on preparing children for transfer to secondary school, the evidence of a sharp increase in maladaptive motivational style in the first year of secondary education might cause surprise and disappointment.

At this point it is worth recalling that our conception of motivational style is essentially qualitative. It moves away from quantitative measures such as time on task and measurable aspects of personality. Attribution theory emphasises the importance of a cognitive process: children decide on the factors to which they should attribute the causes of things they experience at school (and elsewhere). Similarly, the concepts of mastery orientation, learned helplessness and self-worth motivation are based on children making a qualitative judgement about what goals are worthwhile and attainable. Yet in our project we have used quantitative techniques to investigate this essentially qualitative way of understanding motivation.

We must therefore pause and ask what these methods can do, *and* what they cannot. What they have done is elucidate the importance of context in motivational style, notably the subject context, English or mathematics, and the school context, primary or secondary. They have also enabled us to compare groups of pupils, notably boys and girls, Asian and European pupils and different ability and attainment groups. This is all 'broad-brush' stuff, and could not have been done with the use of more intensive qualitative techniques based on a much smaller sample. We felt that this broad-brush approach was necessary in view of the remarkable dearth of systematic information about the motivational responses of pupils in ordinary schools, and in particular the dearth of evidence on how pupils who may be difficult to teach actually react in the face of demanding tasks.

Nevertheless our procedures also contained some notable limitations. The motivation theorists who developed the concepts of mastery orientation, learned helplessness and self-worth motivation, as well as those of task orientation, ego orientation and work avoidance, made assumptions about children's cognitive processes. Many of these assumptions were supported by empirical research but the research was based on the questions the psychologists themselves had developed. What we have not so far been able to do is comment on whether the pupils who took part in our project saw the tasks we gave them in the ways assumed by the theoretical work on which the tasks were based. This, however, raises an additional question, namely whether there may be problems in current ways of thinking about motivation which might be elucidated by asking children to tell us about their understanding of the tasks we had given them.

The importance of children's accounts

Atkinson's early work argued that children's motivational responses arose largely from personality characteristics which remain stable across different contexts (Atkinson, 1964; Atkinson and Raynor, 1974, 1978). Thus, anxiety, helplessness and determination to succeed were all seen as products of underlying personality traits which would be relatively stable and unresponsive to interventions aimed at changing motivational style. Clearly, Atkinson's theory would not have predicted the importance of the subject context, nor of transfer to secondary school. More recent theories have placed far greater emphasis on cognitive processes involved in motivation. Children are recognised as active in the development of their own learning styles, albeit in the context of the formative influence exerted by variables in their learning environment.

Weiner's (1974, 1984, 1986) work was a notable advance in understanding motivation with its focus on four categories or types of cause generally represented by luck, ability, effort and the difficulty level of the task itself. Essentially, Weiner represents motivational style in terms of information processing. This sees the motivational style a pupil adopts as the outcome of the pupil's exposure to particular patterns of information. On this model, motivational style develops as the pattern of information becomes more clearly established and begins to interact with the attributional process in order to produce a consistent and repeated response. Weiner argues that the experience of failure over a long period will give rise to different attributions to those produced by the experience of success. For instance where a child consistently experiences high achievement despite low levels of effort it is likely that the child's attributions for that success will be to high ability. Similarly, where high effort on a task perceived to be difficult results in failure the attribution is likely to be one of lack of ability. The fact that the child's attributions are seen as choices, made from a range of possible interpretations, suggests that if changes can be made to the pattern of information given to the student about his or her performance then corresponding changes will occur in that student's attributional responses. However, the possibility of successful intervention will, on Weiner's model, largely turn upon the degree to which informational and attributional patterns have become entrenched. This suggests that responses will become more stable, and therefore that the success of intervention will be less, as a child grows older.

Yet although Weiner's approach was an advance on the personality-bound theories which preceded it, he does not offer a convincing explanation for our results. In particular the differences in rates of maladaptive motivational style between subjects, together with the impact of school, teacher and department variables suggests that motivational style is not influenced only by patterns of information *over a long term.* Weiner recognises that quite short-term changes in context, such as a new teacher or a new school may also have an effect, but his model may be criticised for two more general reasons. First, there is mounting evidence to suggest that his model may be too narrow to represent accurately the complexity of the attributional process. In particular the strategic character of students' actions and explanations are obfuscated by the simplicity of traditional attributional matrices. Secondly, despite efforts made by more recent researchers to acknowledge the extent and significance of diversity within the attributional process, there are theoretical grounds for adopting an alternative model that places emphasis upon the goal-directed behaviour of students and the strategic character of their responses to learning events and contexts (Dweck, 1991).

Mastery orientation and learned helplessness are attributional analyses of children's responses to difficult or challenging tasks. Self-worth motivation has a different theoretical basis, but it is nevertheless a cognitive response to a challenging task. What these motivational styles have in common is that they are goal directed. On the other hand, they suffer from the same limitations as attribution theory. In order to move our understanding of motivational processes forward, it was becoming clear that we needed to see how children themselves understood the tasks we had given them.

Kelley and Michela (1980) argued that the central irony of attribution theory lay in the lack of research that had, up to then, been undertaken into the causal distinctions which people themselves make in providing explanations of their success and failure. The rigidity of the attributional model may actually reflect the categories which psychologists have imposed on children's meanings. In other words, they may be the psychologist's meanings conceived out of dominant traditions within psychology and not the meanings used by children in their interpretation of the world and their behaviour (Little, 1985). This distinction is important because it challenges the assumption implicit in traditional attribution theory which maintains that attributional choices are made in response to externally provided information.

Craske's technique is clearly open to this criticism; it was designed to place children in one of three motivational styles. Nicholls' distinction between task orientation, ego orientation and work avoidance is also open to the same criticism; pupils' responses are inevitably constrained by the contextual design of the questionnaire. Evidence of children developing and applying their own attributional categories (Frieze *et al.*, 1983) suggests that they are proactive in creating the conditions under which certain challenges or threats have a meaning. Thus, a learned helpless orientation on Craske is based on the theoretical assumption of a self-perceived lack of ability: 'I can't do this.' However, the identification of learned helplessness has little meaning without evidence about how the child perceives the significance of the test and the consequences of a particular outcome. What is interpreted from a test as learned helplessness may actually be a lack of interest in what is construed as a pointless exercise: 'There's no point. I can't do this.' The interaction between the child and learning context in which choices are made is critical to an understanding of a child's decisions. Similarly, a response categorised as self-worth motivation is based on the theoretical assumption that ability is important in Western culture. Yet for individual pupils, maintaining their position in a peer group of pupils for whom goals set by the school appear irrelevant to their future needs may be far more important.

In other words, when we identify specific motivational styles, we are using children's responses to make assumptions about their attributions which may not be borne out if we actually talk to them. This becomes clear if we look again at the notion of ability which plays such a central role in the culture of modern Western society. Just as it is more useful to think of self-concept in terms of different aspects of the self, for example physical or academic self-concept, than as a global concept, so most of us understand the meaning of ability in different ways depending on the time and context. Thus, whilst a student may at one time have an entity view of ability which assumes he/she has no control over ultimate levels of achievement, at another the same student may have an incremental view of ability which holds ability to be extendible through the process of learning itself. This has led Dweck (1991) to argue that in exploring student motivation it is important to consider the view individuals have of the nature of their own ability, their goal orientation, and their level of confidence in their present ability. Dweck sees motivational style as consistent over time and context only so long as the child's beliefs and goals themselves hold constant. Thus, she argues that in examining differences in motivational style it is important to consider how children's goals are related to the learning environment, including such things as the form of assessment used in the classroom as well as the interactions between teachers and students. This view implicitly acknowledges the negotiable character of ability in our society. The possibility that people operate with different conceptualisations of ability at different times in their lives suggests that they are actively engaged in defining these culturally important notions.

However, it is not really sufficient merely to emphasise the dominant position accorded to notions of ability or achievement in our society. One needs also to be aware of how particular conceptions of ability are reached at particular times, together with the circumstances in which conceptions of ability are reproduced and resisted. Dweck's approach does not entirely free motivational theory from the constraints of a rigid attributional mode. It remains tied to an assumption that children's motivation is framed within the context of a fairly narrow set of relationships defined by psychologists. This assumption is misleading because it takes for granted certain cultural representations of concepts such as 'ability' and 'success'. Dweck fails to consider how attributional processes operate to construct and contest the meanings attached to these concepts in people's lives. To overcome these problems we need to explore children's understanding of the tasks they are set in greater depth than is possible with a battery of Craske-type tests or a questionnaire. To do this we needed to talk with them.

Interviews with children

Aims and procedure

Our aims at this stage of the project were to gain an understanding of the attributional processes which might be behind some of the results described in Chapters 4–6. We wanted to throw light on children's understanding of the test battery we had given them and to offer a perspective on motivational style which might complement the other information we had collected without being restricted to the three motivational styles identified by Craske's technique. It followed from these aims that the interviews with children would focus on their reactions to the four tests, but that we were not using the interviews to investigate the validity of Craske's procedure for identifying motivational style. Consequently, we would not be trying to 'triangulate' information from the tests with information from the interviews.

The interview schedule itself was short, and focused explicitly on children's reactions to each of the four tests. Because we were not at this stage interested in comparisons between subjects, we asked pupils only about the mathematics tasks. Each interview lasted about ten minutes. Given the limited time available, we concentrated our efforts on Year 6, for two reasons. First, Year 6 had a higher proportion of mastery oriented children; given their lower levels of maladaptive motivational styles than in subsequent years, we wanted to see what children in Year 6 would tell us about the demands which they felt the four tests had made on them. Second, information from Year 6 children would form a necessary basis for comparison in future interview-based work with older pupils.

We identified 51 children from the 11 primary schools. Selection was based on the need for a sample which included the different styles of motivation identified by the tests. For this reason, the interviews took place after the children had completed all four tests, and the majority were completed within two weeks of the fourth test. Of the 51 children, 21 were girls and 30 boys.

Perceptions of overall performance

Little (1985) found that children frequently responded to causal questions with a description of the outcome. At first sight these sorts of responses might appear uninteresting in that they do not reveal the reasoning underlying the child's description of a particular outcome. Little gives the example (footnote, p. 12) of the child who responds to the question 'What is the reason X is working well?' by answering 'He gets all his sums right'. In Little's opinion these descriptive accounts require further probing to ascertain from the child an explanation of that outcome. Although not wishing to reject this view entirely, we did find in our interviews that where children gave descriptive accounts of their performance these could be very revealing. These descriptions often suggested that a general sense of emotional 'well-being' or 'discontent'

Table 7.1 **Perception of overall performance (N=50 children responding)**

Category	Example	Frequency of responses
Focus on task		
Performance	'I did some a bit wrong', 'I could have done better'	5
Task difficulty	'The tests were hard', 'The tests got harder'	4
Time	'I didn't have enough time to finish'	2
Effort	'I tried my best'	1
Specific competence	'I'm good at maths'	1
Interest	'I don't like maths'	1
Focus on affect		
Task achievement	'I did quite good', 'Not very good'	23
Comparison with self	'Better than I usually do'	12
Comparison with others	'Better than my friends', 'Same as my friends'	4

was more significant *for the child* than any particular explanation of the reasons for that outcome. Thus Little's assumption that a descriptive response to a causal question is the product of the child's lack of sophistication in framing answers to causal questions may be somewhat misleading. For instance Table 7.1 shows the type of responses offered by children in our sample when questioned about their overall performance on the four tests we gave them. We have grouped the responses under two headings, according to whether the child's explanation focused on the task itself or on her/his affective reaction to the task. Just over a quarter of the accounts were task focused (14) and related to such things as task performance (5), task difficulty (4), the time available to do the tests (2), etc. The majority of the accounts, however, focused upon the children's affective reaction to their performance of the tasks (39). By looking at the actual responses these children made to the question rather than forcing them into explanatory categories we can see that in the overall evaluation of their performance what mattered was not the reasons for a particular outcome but rather an evaluation of how that outcome affected them personally.

This became more apparent when we asked children for further explanations of possible differences between their actual performance and what they had hoped to achieve. Although nine children maintained that there was no gap between their actual and wished for levels of achievement, 22 responses focused on the emotional consequences of such outcomes (e.g. 'I'm ashamed when I don't do as well as I expect of myself') and 14 on effort (e.g. 'I feel that I should have worked harder'). These accounts are important because they indicate what for these children was important about their own performance.

The strength of this emotional reaction to the experience of success or failure on classroom tasks may be overlooked where questioning focuses on children's attributions for success and failure. When we turned to children's attributions in respect of their performance on Test 1, 50 out of 59 responses focused on specific aspects of the task (e.g. 'it was quite easy' or 'I didn't understand some questions'). The emphasis placed upon task attributions is quite striking and contrasts sharply with the type of attributions volunteered by children in respect of their perform-ance on later tests in the sequence. In part the emphasis placed upon task difficulty rather than upon performance may be explained by the fact that at this stage direct comparisons of performances on different tests were not requested. It is also noteworthy that none of the children, when interviewed about their performance on this test, made reference to effort attributions.

Children's attributional statements in respect of their performance on Test 2 showed quite a different picture to that revealed for Test 1. Here, despite a significant increase in the difficulty of the test, its dif-ficulty was rarely referred to as an explanation of particular outcomes. Major emphasis was placed instead upon the emotional implications of the outcome (33 out of 45 responses, e.g. 'I was disappointed' or 'I felt bad') rather than upon the causal explanation of this. The move is towards explanations of performance which focus upon the sense of negative affect, i.e. disappointment, or shame, etc., which the outcome engendered. Even though the children appeared to appreciate that the test was significantly harder than Test 1, they tended not to refer to the increased difficulty of the task, preferring instead to concentrate on how they felt about their results. What is particularly important about these responses is that the children's standardised scores were only five marks lower on Test 2 than Test 1 (an average of 9 compared with 14).

This raised two questions. First, were the children reacting to the test itself, or to feedback on their performance; and second, what effect might there be on their feelings about attempting a third test? We investigated the first question by asking the children about their initial perceptions of Test 2. This suggested that the majority had been unaffected by the apparent increase in difficulty, and that it had only given rise to concern *once they had received feedback about their performance.*

When asked how they had felt about the prospect of doing a further test after being told about their score on Test 2, 34 out of 45 children expressed confidence about their future performance.

When we asked children how they had approached Test 3, over half of them gave replies which indicated that they had been thinking strategically about how they should tackle the test on the basis of the experience gained on Tests 1 and 2, for example going slower or faster. This supports the view that the general improvement in performance which some children showed over the sequence of the tests may be accounted for by a 'practice effect'. However, the evidence from these interviews is that this 'practice effect' should not be seen as under- mining the validity of the test procedure adopted in the research. For the 'practice effect' to be operative depends entirely upon children thinking strategically about their performance over the sequence. In other words, the important consideration here is not whether children can improve their performance by practice but rather whether or not they actually adopt an approach towards the task which allows them to use this experience strategically to improve their performance on subsequent tests.

When we questioned children about the reasons for their scores on Test 3 there was a noticeable shift back to explanations in terms of task difficulty compared with responses to the same question in respect of Test 2. These attributions are largely accounted for by those children who identified Test 3 as less difficult than Test 2. Not all children believed this test to be easier than Test 2 and many also believed it to be harder than Test 1. Although it is not possible to draw any strong conclusions on the basis of such a small number of responses, there was, in these cases at least, a relationship between perception of an increase in difficulty on Test 3 and a learned helpless profile on the test battery. However, none of the children we interviewed referred to their ability as a factor affecting their performance on this test. Six children did refer to their way of doing the test as a significant factor affecting their score on the test and a further four children put down their (improved) performance to an increase in confidence based upon familiarity with the type of items used in the tests. For 17 children this strategic adapta- tion was fairly limited, being confined to general effort-based or time- focused strategies. It is arguable whether references to increasing effort can legitimately be identified as embodying genuine strategic responses. However, the time-focused strategies are more clearly suggestive of chil- dren modifying their performance on the basis of expectations based on past experience. In addition eleven children identified more sophistic- ated strategies for improving their performance, including 'thinking', 'checking' and 'ordering' strategies. '

Strategic thinking was not confined to children with mastery profiles on our tests. On the basis of a small sample it is not possible to make general claims about the relationship between strategic thinking and particular motivational styles which had been established on Craske's technique or Nicholls' questionnaire. However, our evidence does suggest that the use of strategies is not simply a reflection of a particular motivational style but rather that children use a variety of motivational styles strategically to construct and contest explanations for their performance.

We asked children if they had changed their way of tackling Test 4 on the basis of feedback about their performance on Test 3. We found that feedback on Test 2 had exerted a greater influence on the children's strategy for tackling Test 3 than the feedback on Test 3 had exerted on Test 4. For the latter, 20 of the 36 replies indicated that they did not expect to make any changes, and only six children referred to changes which involved more specific strategies aimed at improving their performance on the next test.

It was also instructive to compare attributions for performance on Test 4 with those on Test 2. The pattern was very different, with a large majority of 'helpless' responses following Test 2 (e.g. 'I felt bad'), and a large majority of responses referring to effort and strategy following Test 4 (e.g. 'I tried my best because I wanted a higher mark'). These differences might be explained by the information given to children about these different tests. They were given no information by the researcher about the difficulty level of Test 2. The interviewers did not confirm the evaluations the children themselves had made about this test being more difficult than Test 1. Immediately prior to commencing Test 4, however, the researcher had informed the children that they might find this test more difficult than the others. This information gave children an external measure against which to evaluate their performance. The evidence here is that external information influenced many children's evaluation of their performance, even where their orientation was towards mastery. Moreover, it also seems to be the case, for these children at least, that in the absence of explicit, externally defined expectations about performance in relation to task difficulty there was a strong tendency to locate poor performance on a difficult task within the person, rather than making attributions to the difficulty of the task. This does not imply that children are making attributions to lack of ability; rather it suggests their feelings of uncertainty in this situation. The distinction is important because the children were not making a causal connection between their performance and their ability but rather an emotional statement about how their score on the test made them feel about their performance. This seemed to be as much the case for children whose test profiles indicated mastery orientation as it was for children with maladaptive profiles. They were not primarily concerned with why they got the score that they did, but with how that score had made them feel. Reports by children of their initial perceptions of Test 2 suggest that many were unaffected by the apparent increase in difficulty of the test and that this only gave rise to concern once they had received feedback about their performance.

Conclusions

In considering the relationship between motivation and the cultural reproduction of 'success' and 'failure', it is necessary to locate particular psychological processes within their cultural context. By so doing we may also be able to understand better how the reproduction and subversion of achievement orientations occur. In Chapter 6 we saw how the changing context of pupils' lives as they moved from Year 7 to Year 11 might influence the value they place upon academic tasks with important implications for their motivational responses. Thus, what for some students appeared to be learned helplessness might be explained in terms of their rejection of the culture of schooling and their subversion of the goals associated with that culture. In other words it is possible that they no longer cared whether they were perceived to be failing in school because they had rejected the values promoted within school. By contrast with older pupils our evidence from the testing of Year 6 children clearly points to the predominance of mastery orientation profiles. This suggests that these children are relating positively towards the curriculum and the feedback they receive. Yet, these data tell us little about how the differences between Year 6 and Year 11 students come about. It may be the case that there are qualitatively significant differences in the experiences these students have of schooling.

The lack of attention given by psychological theories to culture as a mediating influence between individuals on the one hand and the tasks and settings in which attributions are made on the other is problematic. This is especially so in respect of cross-cultural generalisations but is also the case within a single culture where the homogeneity of attributional systems is often simply assumed. What may be seen as evidence of maladaptive motivational style by researchers and teachers may, from the child's own point of view, represent a meaningful strategy in pursuit of quite rational goals. Frieze *et al.* (1983) have pointed out that while there is a vast literature on the determinants of 'success' and, to a lesser extent, research interest in what students perceive to be the determinants of their own success or failure:

little consideration has been given to the epistemologically prior question of how students decide that a particular performance . . . is a success or failure. (Frieze *et al.*, 1983, p. 3)

This is not to deny the central role given to the concept of 'achievement' in our culture, but there is a problem in the research on student motivation in that it often appears uncritically to assume that the dominant model of achievement is the only one that matters, thereby ignoring the different layers of meaning that this shrouds.

'Ability' is a contentious concept, not just in the discourse of psychology but in the everyday world of human interactions. Notions of 'ability' play an important role in the construction and reproduction of social power, as they also do in processes of exclusion. 'Ability' is a form of cultural capital that is nurtured and protected by some whilst offering opportunities for social mobility to others. However, lack of 'ability' and 'failure' to achieve not only exclude people from systems of reward but also legitimise their lack of opportunity in the world. In investigating motivational styles and attributional statements researchers need to be aware of this wider social context within which their categories are located and by which they are made meaningful to students.

Evidence of conflict over values between working-class students and their schools has been available for a long time (Hargreaves, 1967; Willis, 1977; Davies, 1982). Willis' 'lads' showed a very profound, if not fully articulated, understanding of something that researchers may fail to recognise. Classroom tasks have different and at times contradictory meanings. These tasks are also underpinned by assumptions about the character of 'knowledge' and its social value. For instance, whose knowledge it is; what social and cultural significance can be attached to the privileging of certain kinds of 'knowledge' or ways of 'knowing'? It is more than a little naive to assume that children's responses to classroom tasks are framed only by the task or by the classroom processes that form its immediate context. These processes may, however, become the ground upon which meaning and control are reproduced and contested by children and their teachers alike, culminating for some children in the experience of alienation being galvanised during the final school years through the culture of the peer group into a rejection of school values. Willis' lads were highly motivated towards finding an identity within their own communities. Their sense of self-worth was maintained by membership of a peer group that explicitly rejected classroom success. The deconstruction of classroom 'success' by these young people was implicit in a social practice which rejected what for them was an abstract and offensive individualism.

It is unlikely that changes like this suddenly just happen. For some children they are the outcome of the accumulated experience of what Spindler (1987) has called the 'long degradation of schooling'. The apparently highly motivated pupils in our primary school sample had not yet reached the stage where academic failure was experienced as social alienation. However, our interviews did reveal something of the complexity of the experience of school when viewed from the perspective of children themselves. These children were beginning to see themselves in new ways as their awareness of the social and cultural implications of educational success and failure grew. Yet for the majority of children this awareness was still contained within the boundaries of an overall mastery orientation towards learning in school. By Years 9 and 11 when our quantitative data suggest a considerable increase in maladaptive orientations, the strategic thinking that was evident in Year 6 may have begun to serve a wider set of goals arising out of the growing maturity of the children's perceptions of the nature and limits of opportunity structures within their schools. The strategic uses of attributions that we found among our Year 6 pupils may suggest how 'failure' is understood in terms of its social implications and therefore how 'mastery' orientations come to be rejected by those who feel themselves to have most to lose. In these circumstances, despite being counter-productive as a learning strategy, self-worth concern and even learned helplessness are entirely rational. A mastery orientation may be a luxury that only the 'successful' can afford to adopt. Whereas teachers and researchers focus their attention on improving learning opportunities, children may themselves operate from a more realistic assessment of the discriminatory role played by narrow conceptions of 'achievement' and 'success' as measures of personal worth in our society.

PART THREE

Influencing motivation

CHAPTER EIGHT

Influencing motivation: children, their goals and their schools

Introduction

It will be clear by now that the concept of motivation is imprecise. In spite of the near universal agreement on its importance, few clear messages have come across to teachers from an extensive body of research. Motivation remains as slippery, elusive – and important – as other widely used terms such as self-esteem and self-concept. Perhaps, though, its elusiveness and its importance are related. If motivation was easy to understand, raising it would be correspondingly easy and neither teachers nor psychologists would need to spend time worrying about it. Motivation is intrinsically linked to the debate about raising educational standards; if there were no debate about standards there would be none about motivation, but as long as there is controversy about how to raise standards there will be controversy about how to raise pupils' and teachers' motivation. It follows that motivation is likely to remain a subject of intense interest to politicians, parents, teachers and the media.

The obvious gaps in our understanding should not blind us to what has been achieved. The results of our own studies support the views developed, mainly, by theorists in North America. Motivation can be positive or negative: pupils can be motivated *not* to attempt a task as strongly as they can to complete it successfully. Similarly, motivational style – the consistent pattern of motivational responses within a given situation – can be adaptive or maladaptive; it can help pupils' learning at school or act as an obstacle to it. In particular, difficult tasks can elicit adaptive or maladaptive reactions. By definition almost, effective learning involves overcoming difficult tasks, so we need to consider the implications for school and classroom organisation and for teaching methods. It is also clear that individuals *decide* how to act, and their decisions vary from situation to situation. One of the most dramatic examples of this is the way in which behaviour, quality of work, and motivation, can vary as secondary school pupils move from one lesson to another. In other words, personality does not determine a pupil's motivation – contextual influences are also critically important.

In the final part of this book we analyse the implications of our own work and of other research for the goals schools set themselves both at institutional and at classroom level. In the next chapter we will focus on the implications for school and teacher effectiveness, but before moving to these wider implications we need to summarise our own evidence and to focus on the implications of motivation research for understanding pupils as individuals. In particular, we will examine the role of individual differences in motivational style, and link this with the contextual influences which our research has shown to be important. We shall argue that not only are the influences on motivation multivariate, but so are motivational responses. We will evaluate what our results tell us about the difficult to teach, with particular reference to the large minority in Britain who historically have been regarded as having special educational needs. As a consequence of that evaluation we will re-examine the relationship between the confused notion of ability and special educational need. That will lead to a discussion of the roles of failure and of effort in understanding motivation. Finally we will argue that although our results are consistent with a theory of motivation based on the goals individuals set themselves, there are notable limitations in this approach which can only be resolved by integrating research on motivation with research on school and teacher effectiveness.

Influences on motivational style: an overview

It is clear from our brief survey of teachers' perceptions of their pupils that they see pupils with learning and/or behavioural difficulties as being particularly difficult to motivate. This does *not* mean that only these pupils have motivational problems, but it does imply that teacher attention focuses on them. The immediate question is whether this perception is justified. The evidence in Chapter 4 suggests that it may be. Children with low non-verbal reasoning and low educational attainments were more likely to show maladaptive motivational styles in Years 7 and 9 than pupils in high bands. By Year 11 this was not apparent, but they tended to have lower scores in task orientation and ego orientation on Nicholls' (1989) motivational orientation scale, at least in mathematics. What is equally clear, though, is that it was not only pupils with low non-verbal reasoning and low educational achievements who were identified as learned helpless or self-worth motivated. Moreover there were pupils in these special educational needs groups who were identified as mastery oriented. In other words, we are talking about a substantial amount of overlap between groups.

We found few significant differences in motivational style adopted by girls and boys, or by pupils in Asian and White communities. There was a tendency for more Asian girls to be mastery oriented than Asian boys, but overall these individual characteristics seemed much less important than aspects of the school system and the classroom. Thus, there was a highly significant increase in maladaptive motivational style in the first year of secondary schooling, with a corresponding drop in mastery orientation. In Years 9 and 11 there was evidence of a swing back towards mastery orientation, but not to the level observed in the final year of primary schooling. The most consistent and most striking result, though, was between English comprehension and aspects of mathematics. Mastery orientation was more evident in the latter in every year group, for boys and girls, for pupils of every NVR or attainment band, and for European and Asian pupils. In addition to this evidence of subject-related differences, we found some evidence of a school effect, with a tendency for higher rates of mastery orientation at Summertown School than Springtown. We also found evidence of differences between teachers in the number of mastery oriented pupils in their classes, at least in secondary schools.

A central point throughout is the variability in responses. Some Band 1 pupils were identified as learned helpless or self-worth motivated and some Band 4 pupils as mastery oriented. Similarly, our results only showed a *tendency* towards mastery orientation in aspects of mathematics compared with English comprehension. The interviews with Year 7 pupils were useful here, drawing attention to children's emotional reactions to the tests for identifying motivational style. These not only confirmed the variability which was evident from the quantitative analysis but also provided grounds for challenging some of the dominant thinking about motivation, notably with regard to the concept of ability.

A second central point from our results is that although individual differences are important, they cannot provide the whole picture. Understanding motivation is *not* just about understanding individual differences in response to a given set of experiences, tasks and teaching methods at school. Teachers also need to explain and analyse how the organisation and delivery of these experiences, tasks and teaching methods influence the motivational styles which individual pupils adopt. In other words, individual differences are important, but so is the interaction between them and contextual influences.

Individual and contextual differences

In the 1960s personality theory exerted a dominant influence on psychology. One of the reasons for it running into a blind alley, and consequently losing much of its popularity, was that it failed to predict with any degree of accuracy the things in which practitioners were interested, for example delinquency or academic success. Motivation theory faces a similar problem, though Dweck and Bempechat (1983) seek to make a virtue of it:

it has been a continual source of interest to us that the tendency to display the facilitating or debilitating pattern in the face of difficulty appears to be virtually independent of the child's level of ability – either as assessed by such standardised measures as IQ or achievement tests, or by measures of task performance prior to encountering obstacles. (p. 240)

In our own research, though, the Dweck and Bempechat's 'debilitating patterns' were *not* 'virtually independent of the child's level of ability'. They were significantly more common in pupils with low NVR and low educational achievements. In common with a very high proportion of motivation research, the samples to which Dweck and Bempechat were referring were small, selected either from clinical populations or, more frequently, from 'normal' children for the purposes of controlled small-scale experiments. In contrast our study focused on all pupils in three year-groups at two secondary schools, with a further primary school sample, and this enabled us to see the pattern of responses more clearly than is possible with the dominant small-scale and more tightly controlled methods.

It is nevertheless clear that other influences are even more important than these individual differences. One is the structural change from primary to secondary school. It is not plausible to attribute this to developmental factors as some authors have done (see Chapter 6). If that were the case, we might expect to see gender differences in the first year of secondary schooling (Year 7, or age 11–12 in our sample), in view of gender differences in the age of the onset of puberty. We found no such differences. Clearly, it is the fact of transfer that matters for many children, even if we cannot be specific about the precise features which are important. Other influences are the nature of the tasks pupils are given in different curriculum subjects, the school they are attending and the teacher who happens to be teaching them.

An analogy with IQ is helpful in understanding the role of individual differences in motivation. IQ is associated with different levels of educational achievement, but it is not the only influence on educational achievement. Indeed, within moderately broad IQ bands its predictive power reduces virtually to zero. It is only when the full range is examined that a broad relationship with achievement becomes apparent. Similarly, measures of intelligence such as non-verbal reasoning and measures of educational achievement are only related to motivational style if we take the whole range of achievement. Within any one intelligence or achievement band there is no consistent pattern. In other words, while individual differences in measured intelligence or in educational achievement are important, individual responses to a particular task or situation are equally important.

Another way of understanding this relationship is through an analogy with research on school effectiveness. This research has *not* shown that home background and children's achievements when they enter a school have no influence on their progress and on their educational achievements on leaving. On the contrary, a careful reading of every major study shows that the 'input variables' of home background and achievements on entry are strongly related to subsequent progress and achievements. What the research has shown, however, is that the input variables are not the only influence on subsequent progress. The school also makes a difference. Similarly, in the case of motivation individual differences are important, particularly those associated with the extended concept of special educational need advocated in the Warnock Report and accepted in the 1981 and 1993 Education Acts, but school-related factors also play an important role in influencing pupils' responses.

Multivariate influences and responses

Our research has drawn on several different ways of understanding motivation. The concept of self-worth motivation is based on an assumed need to maintain self-esteem, and therefore comes from a different theoretical tradition to those of mastery orientation and learned helplessness which arise from the factors to which pupils attribute their experiences at school. We have also drawn on Nicholls' (1989) distinction between task orientation, ego orientation and work avoidance, and on De Charms' (1976) notions of 'origins' and 'pawns'. At a theoretical level these distinctions are important. Our interest, in this book, though, has been mainly in evaluating the usefulness of research on motivation for teachers rather than in making a substantial theoretical advance. There is no longer any doubt that much of the early research underestimated the range and complexity of influences on motivation. Atkinson's (1964) early work, for example, was overly deterministic in its emphasis on the role of personality. Yet a similar criticism can be levelled against some of the more recent work arising from attribution theory. As noted in Chapter 7, little of this was based on consistent empirical evidence about the causes to which children or adults actually attribute their success or failure in naturalistic situations (Kelley and Michela, 1980). In consequence of such criticisms, recent work has tended to see motivation in terms of a person's goals. Thus, motivation is increasingly coming to be seen as the product of interaction between individuals and an unlimited range of experiences in their environment. These experiences result in goals, either to achieve a specific end, or simply to maintain a general sense of well-being. In the latter sense, motivation may be seen as having the biological function of maintaining homeostasis.

It follows from this analysis not only that influences on motivation are multivariate, but that motivational responses are also multivariate. Learned helplessness and self-worth motivation may have different origins in motivation theory, but that is an entirely separate point from the usefulness of such concepts in understanding motivation. Similarly, Nicholls (1989), De Charms (1976), and Dweck (1985) each conceptualise motivation in different ways, but each offers a useful framework for making sense of motivation. To return to the analogy with intelligence, there has been extensive debate about what knowledge and skills contribute to the amorphous notion of intelligence, resulting in the tautology that intelligence is what intelligence tests measure. Yet precisely because intelligence is so multifaceted psychologists have developed a wide range of techniques for investigating it. Probably the only things these techniques have in common is that they all attempt to throw light on aspects of human performance, and their usefulness for teachers depends on how far they help in understanding children's learning abilities and educational progress. The same is true of motivation. Techniques for assessing it can be evaluated in terms of their usefulness in helping teachers to understand factors which may help or hinder children's learning. One aspect of this, of course, is recognition of children who, in motivational terms, are difficult to teach.

Who are the difficult to motivate?

We pointed out in Chapter 1 that the 20 per cent or so of pupils regarded by the Warnock Report (DES, 1978) as having special educational needs were characterised mainly by learning or behavioural difficulties which made them difficult to teach. Our own results show that pupils with learning difficulties, associated with low scores on non-verbal reasoning or with low educational achievements, are more likely to show maladaptive patterns of motivational style than other pupils – yet there are many exceptions to this general pattern, and motivational problems are certainly not confined to pupils with low intelligence and / or low achievements. The concept of special educational need is no more precise than that of motivation. Both terms are 'socially constructed' in the sense that groups of people, for example teachers, psychologists or other researchers, have to decide what constitutes evidence of special educational need and of high or low motivation. Using Warnock's criteria, up to 20 per cent of pupils nationally have special educational need, and far more in some schools. Using Craske's procedure we found that well over 50 per cent of all pupils in Years 7, 9 and 11 were showing a maladaptive motivational style in English and only marginally fewer than 50 per cent in mathematics. The limitation with this kind of evidence, both on special educational need and on motivation, is that it is necessarily imprecise. Its strengths are twofold. First, it identifies problems which are widespread and in a literal sense disturbing to teachers. The evidence on prevalence and on the effect on teachers is well known (see Galloway and Goodwin, 1987). Second, and more importantly, it directs attention to the implications for school and classroom practice.

The causal relationship between maladaptive motivational style and pupils being in low achievement bands is not clear. The motivational problem could be caused by low achievement or vice versa. That criticism cannot, however, so easily be put forward in respect of the causal relationship between maladaptive motivational style and low non-verbal reasoning. In so far as non-verbal reasoning measures intelligence, it would be eccentric, to say the least, to claim that maladaptive motivational style causes low intelligence. The reverse – that low non-verbal reasoning causes maladaptive motivation – does not necessarily follow. What we can say with some degree of confidence is that low non-verbal reasoning increases the risk of maladaptive motivational style. Returning to low educational achievement, the relationship is likely to be two-way. Maladaptive motivational style may be a contributing factor in the low educational achievements of some pupils while for others the reverse may apply.

Implications for school policy

Effective education of pupils with special educational needs does not depend on individual educational programmes for all the pupils concerned, in spite of the emphasis on these in the 1993 Education Act. Resources will never permit this, nor could it ever be desirable either on social or on educational grounds. In an influential polemic Hargreaves (1982) provided a sharp critique of 'the cult of the individual'. Schools, he argued, have for so long been obsessed with individual needs that they have overlooked their social function. Personal identity develops in a social context, and if schools do not give their pupils a sense of belonging, with a feeling of being valued as contributing members of a socially cohesive group, they will turn elsewhere to meet this basic human need. The result is seen in disaffected adolescent groups in which members draw strength from their common opposition to the school's norms and culture. As a motivating influence its power can hardly be overestimated.

An educational argument against individual education programmes is that they seldom create opportunities for pupils to learn from each other. In theory an individual programme can be designed to meet a pupil's social needs. In practice the emphasis is all too often on individual progress towards National Curriculum objectives.

The implication of all this is that provision for pupils with special educational needs should be planned as an integral part of the school's overall provision, and not as a bolt-on extra. Simmons (1986) identified three features of a 'whole school' approach to special needs:

(a)   that *all* teachers, not just those primarily concerned with special needs, should be aware of the range of needs that might arise in their classrooms;

(b)   that *all* teachers should be responsible for assessing the difficulties of materials used in their lessons; and

(c)   that *all* teachers should have access to specialised help in dealing, inside the classroom, with children with learning difficulties.

Whole school approaches have attracted extensive attention (e.g. Ainscow and Florek, 1989; Ramasut, 1989). For present purposes, though, the important point concerns their motivational implications. The responsibility given to teachers can create feelings of helplessness if adequate support is not available. Yet individual-based programmes in which children are withdrawn from the classroom for special teaching can also create a sense of helplessness in class teachers: the child has been assessed as requiring special help which by definition they are not qualified to provide. Thus, any form of provision *can* have negative consequences motivationally. In principle, though, offering class and subject teachers support in their work with pupils with learning or behavioural difficulties can be seen as an aid in maintaining their own mastery orientation. In principle, again, it can also send positive messages to pupils, by implying their ability to cope successfully with the mainstream curriculum.

Official thinking on this subject has been characterised by confusion and inconsistency. Among the government's main reasons for introducing the National Curriculum and for subsequent reform, was its determination to raise standards, particularly among the lowest 40 per cent of pupils, whose achievements were low on international comparisons. The National Curriculum with its firm commitment to curriculum entitlement for all pupils was entirely consistent with this view. Low standards were attributed very firmly to an inadequate curriculum, low expectations of pupils' achievements and poor teaching. Yet the 1981 and 1993

Education Acts have adopted a different model. The emphasis is on assessing needs at an individual level and development of individual education programmes. The formal multidisciplinary assessment for pupils with severe or complex difficulties is narrowly individualistic, at least in practice. In an intensive study of the assessment of pupils with emotional and behavioural difficulties, Galloway *et al.* (1994) found that professional reports concentrated on family background and individual tests of intelligence, educational achievement and personality. In no case was there any explicit attempt to evaluate ways in which the quality of teaching and relationships in the classroom might have been reducing or exacerbating the child's difficulties. The problem for teachers is straightforward. Educational rhetoric about individual needs combines with a quasi-official policy in the form of Ofsted's commitment to differentiation between the needs of pupils with different 'ability' levels and the individualistic ethos of the 1993 Education Act to create an unrealistic expectation that not only assessment but also a lot of teaching should take place at an individual level. Both class size and the complexity of the curriculum make this impractical, and to compound the confusion Ofsted policy is also vigorously encouraging whole-class teaching in primary schools in preference to small-group teaching (Ofsted, 1993).

The underlying point in all this is that the quality of teaching for pupils with special educational needs will not be raised by providing increasing numbers of children with individual education programmes. That policy is likely to de-motivate teachers and to convince the pupils themselves that they cannot be expected to learn new skills without special help – hardly the road to mastery orientation or in Nicholls' terms, task orientation. What is needed is policies which support the work of class and subject teachers, enabling them to set realistic goals for the progress of all pupils in their classes.

Precisely the same point applies to motivation. In mainstream schools, special programmes for high-risk groups of pupils are not needed. They have a necessary role in experimental research which aims to disentangle the contextual influences on pupil's motivation, but we are not likely to solve the problems of low motivation in mainstream schools by providing separate programmes aimed at high-risk groups. We know that pupils with special educational needs are a high-risk group, but we also know that aspects of the subject, (in our case English and mathematics), have an even stronger influence on motivational style, irrespective of intelligence or educational achievement, and that structural changes in the school system (primary–secondary transfer), as well as school and teacher variables also have an effect which is not limited to pupils with special educational needs. These arguments imply the need to examine the implications of research on motivation for school and classroom practice. They also raise important questions about the goals which teachers feel able to set children. Central to this position, and to a lot of recent motivation theory, is the concept of ability.

Ability and motivation

The notes for information on the Second Edition of the Cognitive Abilities Test (Thorndike *et al.*, 1986) states:

The Cognitive Abilities Test provides a measure of a child's ability to use and manipulate the three most important means of communication: words, numbers and diagrams. (p. 1)

There are three possible meanings of ability in this sentence. If a child obtains a low score we could mean:

(a) the child has a low achievement level on this set of skills; or
(b) the child has low ability, and this explains why he/she has a low achievement level on this set of skills; or
(c) in spite of the low score, the child does not have low ability and with more effort and/or more teaching could improve her/his score.

The distinctions are fundamental. The first statement is essentially a tautology: a low score shows the child has obtained a low score. No causation is implied. The second and third explanations offer explanations for the low score, in one case closing the possibility of improving performance and in the other leaving it open. Our point is that both in (b) and in (c) ability is independent of achievement. In each case 'ability' refers to a capacity to grasp new skills or a higher level of understanding. In practice it is clear that ability refers to an undefined and global measure of intelligence. When teachers say: 'she has the ability to do better', or 'he is achieving as well as his ability allows' they are making statements about the children's intelligence and its inferred relationship to their academic achievements.

In itself this is not problematic. It becomes problematic in two circumstances. The first is when reference to ability/intelligence is used to explain low achievements and hence to justify making no attempt to raise them. The second is related to this, namely the tendency to conflate ability/intelligence with achievements. This was evident in the quotation above from Thorndike's Cognitive Abilities Tests. Quite clearly, the test does *not* provide a measure 'of a child's *ability* to use and manipulate . . . words, numbers and diagrams'. It provides a measure of how well a child is actually doing these things in comparison with other children. Whether a child has the *ability* to achieve a higher score is another matter altogether which can only be determined by further teaching and subsequent testing.

Attribution theorists have been interested in whether children attribute poor performance to lack of ability or lack of effort. Unfortunately much less attention has been directed at the epistemologically prior, and more important, question whether teachers attribute children's poor performance to lack of ability or lack of effort. This should be a top priority for further research on motivation. Nevertheless the relationship between ability and effort is confused. Teachers and psychologists seldom talk of raising ability through effort, let alone raising intelligence through effort. Effort is conceptually linked to achievement rather than to ability. That, however, presupposes an outmoded concept of intelligence as a global construct which is largely determined genetically. Alternative models emphasise the role of teaching in intellectual development, for example Shayer and Adey's (1992) programme for cognitive acceleration through science education. If this is correct, effort and effective teaching each play a part not only in raising children's achievement level but also in raising the underlying cognitive ability which is needed to raise achievement.

Viewed in this way the question is not whether entity views of ability become more entrenched in adolescence as Nicholls (1989) argues. If that is the case, pupils will increasingly come to attribute prior performance to lack of effort, and we should predict age-related increases in levels of maladaptive motivational styles on Craske's technique. In fact we found a sharp increase in the first year of secondary education, followed by a reduction in Years 9 and 11. Hence, the more important questions are whether teachers' explanations for success or failure on curriculum tasks vary with the age of pupils, and whether pupils themselves use the attributions imposed on them by psychologists and teachers when explaining their own performance.

We were only able to address the second of these questions, and the evidence in Chapter 7 is that children did *not* normally refer to lack of ability in talking about their reaction on finding that they had obtained a substantially lower score on the second test. Instead they emphasised their emotional responses, implying the importance of a global sense of well-being. We therefore need to ask how children's responses are influenced not only by teachers but also by wider cultural and family expectations. Blumenfeld (1992) cites evidence that Japanese children, when asked about their reasons for doing things at school, were more likely than American children to refer to their teachers and their parents. In addition, the Japanese children were more self-critical about failure, and tended to see failure as evidence of the need for greater effort.

Given the confusion in the concept of ability it is not surprising that the pupils we interviewed seldom mentioned it. For a pupil, attribution to his or her own lack of ability could mean:

(a) inability to add to my knowledge or skills because my priorities lie elsewhere; or
(b) inability to add to my knowledge or skills because I could not cope with the intellectual demands.

The first would be a self-worth motivated response and the second a learned helpless one. The evidence, though, suggests that the dominant reaction to a difficult task was neither of these but rather a feeling that their sense of well-being was threatened by their performance on a difficult task. In motivational terms, then, attention should focus on defining the role of effort and the not unrelated role of failure.

Effort and failure

One reason for the preoccupation with self-esteem in teaching children with special educational needs is their teachers' recognition of their all too frequently long history of educational failure. Repeated failure leads to a feeling of helplessness and is destructive of self-esteem. Effort, though, is a 'double-edged sword': the harder we try the more we feel let down if we do not succeed; and if we do not succeed in a task which other people find easy the effect is compounded.

Attribution retraining programmes tend to encourage pupils to attribute failure to lack of effort rather than to lack of ability (cf. Dweck and Goetz, 1978). This is fine as long as increased effort is followed by success rather than by further failure. It is one thing to ensure this in controlled experimental studies but quite another to ensure it in a busy class with more than 30 pupils. Butler (1994) has argued that

Teachers rarely provide clear information either about the fact of poor performance (see reviews by Brophy, 1985; Eccles and Wigfield, 1985) or about its causes (Blumenfeld *et al.*, 1983). Moreover while it is safe to assume that teachers often express anger in the classroom, it is difficult to imagine situations where they will tell failing students directly that they feel sorry for them, as in controlled studies. (p. 278)

We could add that it is also safe to assume that children often encounter tasks which they find difficult and on which they will not succeed at the first attempt. Indeed, this is wholly desirable. A consistent theme in the literature on effective teaching is that it should be intellectually challenging. By definition, tasks which are intellectually challenging are not easy to complete successfully and therefore carry the risk of failure. It is important to note here that the concept of intellectually challenging teaching is independent of the concept of ability *and* of pupils' current achievement levels. It is as important for the pupils in Band 4 in the research reported in Chapters 4–7 as for the pupils in Band 1. There are two implications, one for classroom practice and the second, perhaps more important and certainly more controversial, for school policy.

The implication for classroom practice is that failure must be re-defined, so that it is not seen as evidence of personal inadequacy but as a necessary part of learning. This, of course, is implicit in the concept of mastery orientation. It implies that teachers will give pupils clear feedback on the reasons for their lack of success in a task and on ways to overcome the difficulty they have experienced. It also implies that the emphasis should be on learning something for its own sake rather than in order to enhance one's own position *vis-à-vis* other pupils: in Nicholls' terms, task orientation rather than ego orientation.

The second implication is less straightforward, and arises from doubts about whether the first is realistic. Psychologists whose research concentrates on tightly controlled studies are seldom well-placed to advise teachers on how to manage their classes. The need to re-define failure as a positive experience is valid as far as it goes, but we must ask how realistic it is. There are two main considerations:

1. Government policy since 1979 has consistently encouraged competition between schools. Parents have been encouraged to compare their own children's progress with those of other children. This ego oriented, competitive philosophy is not intrinsically incompatible with a mastery oriented approach to the experience of failure, but it does presuppose a realistic possibility of making progress. Parents, teachers and pupils who doubt that possibility are likely either to feel helpless or to set themselves alternative goals.

2. In order to benefit from failure on a difficult task we need clear and detailed feedback, and a strategy for mastering it. Most primary school classes contain children with a very wide range of achievements, and there is evidence that the gap gets wider as pupils get older (Reynolds and Teddlie, 1996). In these circumstances, the teachers' task becomes, quite simply, impossible. They have:

    (a) to set different tasks to children with different achievement levels;

    (b) to mark these;

    (c) to provide individualised feedback based on each pupils' performance, with strategies for overcoming any difficulties;

    (d) to monitor the success of strategies they have supported.

And this applies to all nine subjects of the National Curriculum.

Ofsted has criticised the quality of teachers' assessment of pupils' work, their recording of it and their reporting on it to colleagues and to parents. This is known evocatively by the acronym ARR. While there is no doubting the importance of ARR for pupils' motivation, we have to ask whether the low quality of ARR about which Ofsted complain may not result from the number, range and complexity of tasks which teachers are expected to do. This, however, raises wider questions about school and teacher effectiveness to which we turn in Chapter 9.

Conclusions

Ames (1992) has reviewed evidence that aspects of teaching which contribute to pupils' perceptions of mastery orientation may be multiplicative. Our own results are consistent with this view. While non-verbal reasoning and educational achievement contributes to motivational style, so do curriculum organisation, the structure of the school system and the professional practice of individual teachers. The controlled studies on which much of the literature on motivation is based suggest theoretically coherent ways of enhancing pupils' motivation. Whether they take adequate account of the reality of classroom life is another matter.

Blumenfeld (1992) has addressed this problem by contrasting goal theories of motivation with 'constructivist' approaches to learning, and arguing that each can illuminate the other:

Goal theory posits that if teacher practices and structures minimize the focus on ability, students will be active learners willing to exert effort and become more cognitively engaged. Constructivist theory assumes that when teachers stress meaningful learning and scaffold instruction, students will be motivated to reconsider their own understanding, meld prior knowledge and experience with new learning, and develop rich knowledge and thinking strategies to apply to real world problems. (p. 278)

Blumenfeld argues that goal theory and constructivism have different origins, but that each can learn from the other. Thus, it would be useful to test the theoretical assumption that constructivist classrooms could be more likely to foster mastery orientation. For our present purposes, though, the most important point is that constructivist theory is more concerned with the social context of learning in ordinary classes, and the ways in which teachers and pupils jointly construct goals and meanings from curriculum tasks (cf. Marshall, 1992). In view of the consistent differences between the motivational styles we observed in English comprehension and in aspects of mathematics, together with the significant differences between schools and teachers, there is an obvious need to relate evidence about motivation to policy and practice in schools. The more general point, though, is that motivation should not be seen in isolation from the elusive but important notions of good practice and of school and teacher effectiveness. It is to these that we turn in our final chapter.

CHAPTER NINE

Influencing motivational style: school and teacher effectiveness

Introduction

A frustrating feature of school effectiveness research is that it does not lend itself easily to school improvement. If school improvement simply depended on applying the lessons learned from demonstrably successful schools, organisational change would be a tediously mundane matter. In fact it remains probably the greatest challenge for school systems internationally. The problems are both conceptual and empirical. At a conceptual level it is now recognised that Rutter *et al.* (1979) over-simplified school effectiveness in their conclusion that schools which were effective on one outcome were likely to be effective on all others. It is now recognised that a school can be differentially effective, for example in affective and cognitive outcomes, or with high and low ability pupils (Reynolds, 1992). We still know relatively little about the dimensions on which effectiveness can vary, and about ways of recognising them. At a pragmatic level researchers have been more successful in developing complex statistical techniques for measuring effectiveness than in understanding the processes which contribute to it in different areas. Again at a pragmatic level, it is notoriously more difficult to effect change than to describe a school's state, and still more difficult to transfer conclusions from one school to another.

Yet if the application of research on school effectiveness is still at an early stage, research on motivation is at an even earlier stage. Several experimental studies have sought to change children's attributions for success or failure, usually by manipulating the feedback teachers or researchers give them. Thus Dweck (1975) gave two groups of children the same test. They praised one group for their efforts but told the second group that they should try harder. As predicted by an attribution theory model, the second group improved their performance significantly more than the first when given another test. The implication here was that the first group had been encouraged to think they had done as well as could be expected, whereas the second group had been encouraged to think they could do better. This is fine as far as it goes, but classrooms in mainstream schools are infinitely more complex than controlled experiments of this sort imply. The problem does not simply lie in the difficulties in manipulating teachers' feedback to pupils. A much more serious problem is the professional judgement needed in deciding what feedback to give. Simplistic panaceas like attributing failure to lack of effort rather than to lack of ability collapse under the reality that a child may have been making a credible effort on a task that is simply too difficult, or has not yet required the 'scaffolding' techniques for tackling the task in manageable stages, or has missed the relevant lessons through illness.

At the end of Chapter 8 we noted Blumenfeld's argument about the complementary features of motivation theory and constructivist theory. Constructivism is currently exerting a strong influence on the curriculum, notably in mathematics (e.g. Davis and Pettitt, 1995), though there is no prospect of most classes being run on explicitly constructivist principles. The aim of linking theories of teaching with theories of motivation is nevertheless a valid one, and in this chapter our aim is to extend the argument into the areas of school and teacher effectiveness. We will start by identifying some key issues in school effectiveness research and arguing that the motivational questions associated with these have to be seen in the context of wider issues of educational policy both at national and at school level. This will lead us to identify obstacles to mastery orientation, and possible ways of overcoming them. We will show that many of the institutional obstacles to mastery orientation are mirrored in the classroom, and will argue that a motivationally favourable climate cannot be seen in isolation from the values which underpin the school's educational and social culture.

School effectiveness and motivation

Interest in school effectiveness depends on dissatisfaction with how the current system is working: if there were no concern, there would be no interest. By the end of the 1970s structural changes in the economy meant that school leavers with no educational qualifications were likely, in many parts of the country, to be unemployed. Politicians and employers who had previously been perfectly happy for schools to produce one of the highest rates of unqualified leavers at age 16 in Western Europe discovered a commitment to raising educational standards. As the country entered a post-industrial economy, it became increasingly clear that the education system in England and Wales was failing to compete internationally. In particular the achievements of pupils in the lowest 40–50 per cent were becoming a source of increasing concern. Those in the top 20 per cent compared quite well with their counterparts in other European countries and in countries in the Pacific Rim (Reynolds and Farrell, 1996).

Consistent findings from systematic research (e.g. Mortimore *et al.*, 1988) as well as from the more impressionistic surveys of HMI have been:

(a)   that schools vary in their effectiveness on a range of dimensions, to an extent that cannot be explained wholly in terms of differences in their pupil intake;

(b)   that differences in children's progress between teachers within a school, or between departments, in a secondary school tend to be larger than differences between schools;

(c)   that gaps in the achievements of the highest and lowest groups of pupils not only increase with age, but also increase in relation to the gaps in competitor countries (Reynolds and Teddlie, 1996).

Publication of the first major UK study of secondary school effectiveness was warmly welcomed by the government. Naively, politicians and some educationalists assumed that since the twelve schools in the study had received similar funding levels, it would be possible to raise the standards of the least effective schools at least to the level of the average schools, without the need for any extra resources. In addition, the idea of 'encouraging' less effective schools to raise their standard was consistent with an ideology which saw benefits in competition between schools, and within schools in competition between pupils.

Competition between and within schools, though, raises questions about the motivational implications of reforms initiated since 1979. It also raises questions about the motivational implications of the analysis of the ills of the school system. If 40 per cent of pupils, as alleged by Sir Keith Joseph (1983) or 50 per cent as suggested by Scottish HMI (SED, 1978), were under-achieving, did that also mean that they were under-motivated, or showing maladaptive motivational style, in school work? In theory, these pupils might have been highly motivated, but on other educational tasks which they and their teachers considered more important than public examinations and other readily quantifiable measures of achievement in what was to become the National Curriculum. That, however, is ingenuous. None of the evidence from research in the 1960s and 1970s pointed to *selective* under-achievement, with low-achieving pupils highly motivated on non-academic tasks. Rather the evidence pointed and, consistently, still points, to a large minority of pupils who were under-achieving across the board and in addition were likely to be regarded as a high risk for behaviour problems.

Our own evidence is broadly consistent with this view. Pupils with low non-verbal reasoning scores and low achievement scores were a high-risk group for maladaptive motivational style. The causes both of their low achievements and of their maladaptive motivational styles are nevertheless highly complex and cannot usefully be seen in isolation from wider issues of education policy both at national and at school levels, any more than they should be seen in isolation from classroom-level teaching methods.

Obstacles to mastery orientation

Blumenfeld (1992) and Stevenson and Stigler (1992) argued that Japanese pupils were more mastery oriented than their American counterparts; they tended to adhere to 'incremental' theories of ability in Dweck and Elliott's (1983) terms and were more self-critical about failure. Reynolds and Teddlie (1996) offer another perspective on this. Contrasting classes in Britain and North America with Pacific Rim countries, they claim:

American and British thinking reflects a belief in the inherent existence of the normal distribution, or 'bell-curve', with a proportion of children always seen as lying away from the average in the long trailing edge that characterises the normal distribution. In the case of Britain, the nature of the class system and the desire to actively restrict the numbers of talented people to the ranks of already advantaged classes in society has also generated a belief in the inevitability or desirability of failure.

In Taiwan and the other Pacific Rim societies, no such beliefs exist, in spite of the cultural pervasiveness of numerous other ideas and notions imported from America. Education is seen there as a hurdle, which all children can jump in their early years and over which it is the job of the school to push all children, although it is accepted that educational paths later in life may diverge. Classes in the first three or four years of elementary school are mixed ability and indeed one can see entire classes waiting for the last child in the class to work out how to do some problem before the whole class moves on. Teachers move up and down the rows of children correcting the work of the slower learners. Those children will be seen finishing their work at the end of lessons and may also be kept behind at the end of school to ensure that no 'tail' of children differentiates itself from the rest of its peers. (pp. 18–19)

Reynolds and Teddlie go on to point out that most teaching is by whole-class instruction, and eschews differentiated group-work on the grounds that this would increase the range of achievement in the class rather than reduce it.

It is not hard to imagine an Ofsted inspector's reaction to these lessons. Inspectors would be appalled by the lack of differentiation. They would claim that bright children were not being 'stretched'. They would insist that the teaching was insufficiently interactive. These lessons would be rated 'unsatisfactory'; too many of them, and the local press would receive a treat in the form of a failing school. Yet Reynolds' and Teddlie's own work supports other studies which have consistently shown that pupils in Pacific Rim countries out-perform children in Britain in mathematics and science. While no one would suggest that methods from one country could be imported directly to another (although Britain and North America continue to earn huge sums in foreign currency by attracting Higher Education students from countries whose school systems appear, at least in some respects, to be more effective), one is entitled to ask whether Ofsted has an ideological bias against systems which appear – again in some respects – to be highly successful. A more serious point, though, is that the single-minded commitment to mastery of key skills which is evident in the Pacific Rim may result in a narrower curriculum than in Britain and North America with less opportunity to develop artistic and creative skills. Nor is it clear that this system favours the most able children. Alexander *et al.* (1992) described the chronic under-achievement in Britain – Joseph's 'bottom 40 per cent' – as an 'extended tail of distribution'. It is possible that the success of Pacific Rim countries in preventing this 'extended tail' is purchased at the price of 20–30 per cent of pupils at the other end of the achievement continuum. In other words, a system which encourages and rewards excellence may contain as a necessary corollary under-achievement by other pupils who then become labelled as difficult to teach. That is fine in an economy which only needs 20–30 per cent of pupils to have an academic education. If changes in the economy mean that 80–90 per cent of young people need the skills which formerly were required only by 20–30 per cent, it becomes highly problematic.

The implication here is that classroom pedagogy is not just a matter for the professional judgement of teachers. Nor is a commitment to mastery orientation in all pupils. Both pedagogy and, for teachers and for pupils, motivation reflect culturally defined assumptions and priorities. The DFEE's commitment to the gold standard of GCE A level is one such priority. It ensures that 20–30 per cent of eighteen-year-olds achieve a high standard in a small number of subjects. That commitment is not theoretically incompatible with a commitment to raising standards of the lowest 40 per cent, but if the entire system is based on comparisons within schools between high and low sets, and between schools in publication of league tables of examination results, some pupils, and some schools are likely to find the comparisons debilitating. There is little point in motivation theorists urging teachers to encourage pupils to focus on the task rather than on an absolute achievement level when their future status in the school depends on absolute achievement levels.

The literature sometimes reads like an eulogy of task-focused goals, with supreme indifference to the cultural and structural obstacles. Thus Anderman and Maehr (1994) claim that:

Numerous studies have found that students who adopt task-focused (mastery) goals are more likely to engage in deep cognitive processing, such as thinking about how newly learned material relates to previous knowledge and attempting to understand complex relationships. In contrast, students who adopt ability-focused (performance) goals tend to use surface-level strategies, such as the rote memorization of facts and immediately asking the teacher for assistance when confronted with difficult academic tasks. (p. 295)

Yet the organisation of most secondary schools and the competitive nature of the 18+ exam system systematically encourages what Nicholls (1989) describes as ego orientation, in preference to task orientation. In a thoughtful review, Pintrich *et al.* (1993) make the conventional claim that:

evaluation procedures that focus on competition, social comparison and external rewards can foster a performance goal orientation where the learner focuses on besting others rather than gaining a conceptual understanding of the content. (p. 177)

They recognise that:

classroom organization and the nature of many classroom academic tasks may encourage students to get it done, not think it through. . . . (p. 181)

but their solution is:

to create types of authentic tasks or projects without one right answer and with larger periods of time for completion in order to help stave off seeking closure and facilitate more cognitive activity and conceptual change. (p. 181)

While we have no problem with the authors' theoretical analysis, we have to recognise not only that they are demanding a high level of versatility and skill from teachers but also, perhaps more important, that there are powerful constraints on the application of this approach. In England and Wales these constraints include an open enrolment system in which parents are encouraged to choose their child's school, a school funding system based on the number of pupils the school manages to recruit, league tables of results of national testing programmes and individual education programmes for pupils with special educational needs. In other words, the literature is driven by theoretical and philosophical considerations with scant regard to the circumstances in which most teachers have to work and most pupils have to learn.

Overcoming the obstacles

It would be too easy, though, to take a deterministic and 'helpless' view of the cultural and legal obstacles to developing a culture which encourages mastery orientation. An analogy with Bowles and Gintis' (1976) work is useful here. They argued that schools reproduce, and often deepen, the divisions that exist in capitalist society. In this view, teachers are merely the means by which power differentials are maintained; as unwitting agents of the state, they have little or no scope to change the situation. Hargreaves (1982) provided a notable critique of this deterministic argument, claiming that it underestimated the ability of teachers and pupils to define their own meanings in educational activities.

If teachers were merely the passive agents of capitalist society we could not realistically expect to find differences between teachers in pupils' progress or behaviour (e.g. Mortimore *et al.*, 1988), nor in the motivational styles of their pupils, as in our own research. Galloway (1995) has argued that although the school exerts an influence on pupils' progress as well as on their attendance and on the likelihood of them being in trouble with the police, it is a relatively small influence compared with that of the family and the community in which they live. In contrast, the school is the dominant influence on pupils' behaviour while they are actually at school. If this seems surprising, one only has to think about the ways that pupils' behaviour changes with a change of teacher. Home background cannot be blamed if pupils who have been highly motivated to master tasks in a science lesson become inattentive and disruptive five minutes later in a French lesson. Children's behaviour, in other words, is strongly influenced by the immediate characteristics of their environment. Work in schools with exceptionally low rates of problem behaviour suggests very clearly that teachers have a mastery orientated approach to behaviour (e.g. Galloway, 1983). Thus, teachers are themselves expected to deal with problems in their classes rather than referring the pupils concerned to a more senior member of staff. They are, however, expected to seek guidance from experienced colleagues. In other words they are not left to sink or swim, but know that a colleague can advise them about a problem without normally removing their responsibility for solving it.

The contextual influences on pupils' motivation include, obviously, their teachers. Our results showed, however, that the structure of the subject is also likely to be important, as English comprehension was consistently associated with lower rates of mastery orientation than aspects of mathematics. It seems likely that the structure of this subject combines with feedback from the teacher to give pupils a better idea of how they can master a problem than in tasks such as English comprehension.

The teacher strategies which foster mastery orientation with respect to behaviour will not necessarily promote mastery orientation in pupils' learning. Effective behaviour management does not necessarily imply effective classroom learning. In the longitudinal study which preceded *Fifteen Thousand Hours* (Rutter *et al.*, 1979), Rutter (1976) found schools with exceptionally positive behaviour but poor academic standards. One of the four schools with very low rates of disruptive behaviour in Galloway's (1983) study had exceptionally poor exam results, which could not be attributed to the achievements of the pupils on admission. Hence, we have to move from a school-level analysis to that of the classroom.

Teacher effectiveness and motivation

One of the tasks facing pupils at school is to distinguish between rhetoric and reality. This is seldom difficult and is encapsulated in John Nicholls' (1976) choice of title for one of his articles: 'Effort is virtuous, but it's better to have ability'. In many contexts, achievement quite clearly *is* more important than effort, whatever teachers and parents may say. Perhaps it is because they recognise the tensions inherent in schools that teachers sometimes give the confused and confusing messages noted by Dweck and Bempechat (1983):

Some children (the less 'bright' ones) may even begin to label themselves as failures simply because they are consistently assigned easy work, may be praised for work that does not seem particularly noteworthy . . . , or may even receive praise for intellectually irrelevant aspects of their work when the intellectual content is questionable. It may also be the case that when these children do encounter obstacles or commit errors, teachers are apt to gloss over the errors or supply the answer in a well-meant attempt to prevent discomfort. (p. 251)

In achievement orientated cultures you admire the winners and sympathise with the gallant losers – as long as they don't make a fuss. If they do, in the school context, the solution is exclusion and placement in a special unit.

Just as we argued against a negatively deterministic view of school influences, however, we must guard against pessimism about teachers' scope for encouraging a mastery orientated approach in their pupils' learning. Experience of different pupil behaviour with different teachers, together with successive HMI criticisms of unacceptable variation in children's progress between schools and between teachers in the same school, suggests that we should seek a link between teachers' motivational strategies and those of their pupils. The recent motivation literature generally emphasises the importance of effort attributions and the 'well meant attempts to prevent discomfort' noted above by Dweck and Bempechat. Another approach is to review conclusions from work on effective teachers and consider how far this throws light on their motivational strategies.

The notion of motivational style suggests that we might usefully look at the styles of effective teachers in order to investigate motivation in natural classroom settings. However, this has proved a disappointing line of inquiry for three reasons. First, it has been remarkably difficult to identify discrete teaching styles which are used consistently. Second, the links between teaching style and pupils' progress have not been established with any clarity. Third, the differences between teachers adopting any one style are greater than those between styles. In other words, some but not all formal teachers are effective, and the same applies to those adopting a more informal style. Harris (1995) concludes that a mixture of approaches is preferable, depending on the learning task; this conclusion is consistent with HMI calls for teachers to use a variety of approaches.

An alternative approach is to identify features of effective teaching. HMI (1990) identify four features of particular relevance to our argument:

(a) teachers have high expectations which they convey to pupils in a purposeful way;
(b) pupils are given some opportunities to organise their own work;
(c) there is an appropriate match between the pupils' abilities and the tasks they are given;
(d) pupils see lessons as challenging and relevant to their interests, and their interest is maintained.

It is difficult to imagine teachers in the Pacific Rim schools described by Reynolds and Teddlie (1996) being concerned with matching tasks to different ability levels, nor is it their prime concern that pupils should see lessons as relevant to their interests. They certainly would not be preoccupied with other features of effective teaching in Britain.

Like Kyriacou (1991) other writers have highlighted the active or interactive nature of teaching skills. For example Clark and Peterson (1986) note how teachers' effectiveness in the classroom seems, in part, to depend on how well they modify and change their strategies as lessons proceed (Harris, 1995, p. 4). All of these features of effective teaching imply mastery orientation on the part of teachers and pupils alike. Setting high standards with challenging tasks carries the obvious risk of failure, and maintaining pupils' interest demands much higher level skills in the teacher than the sterile call for more effort attributions in some of the attribution theory literature. It may be possible in Pacific Rim countries to motivate pupils by simply telling them to try harder. There is a cultural expectation that everyone will reach a certain standard with powerful sanctions against defaulters, and an enormous amount of time and effort is spent in private tuition outside formal school hours. The variety of learning activities and the development and extension of pupils' language which are seen as part of 'good practice' in Britain have a much lower priority. It seems from this analysis that promoting mastery orientation in children is an infinitely more complex task in Britain than in countries with a more formal system and, perhaps, more limited curriculum. It is beyond this book's scope to consider whether the British system makes unrealistic demands of teachers, and thereby fosters maladaptive motivational styles from them and from their pupils. What is less controversial is that mastery orientation requires a coherent *educational* philosophy. This educational philosophy needs not only to incorporate a theory of learning, as in Blumenfeld's (1992) integration of goal theory with constructivist approaches to learning, but also to recognise aspects of the social context which often remain hidden.

Intellectually challenging teaching is a necessary condition if pupils are to develop mastery orientation: if there is no challenge there is nothing to master. Yet intellectually challenging teaching carries the risk of failure for the pupil. It also carries risks for teachers; these lie in the possibility of loss of control if the class becomes restless, and the possibility of complaints from colleagues and parents. Doyle (1986) argues that teachers and pupils each have a vested interest in negotiating down the intellectual requirements of a task. Pupils benefit because they avoid the sense of discomfort and threat to their self-esteem associated with failure and teachers benefit because a threat to the stability of the class is removed. Teachers and pupils are in a symbiotic relationship, each needing the other's co-operation. Doyle's solution would be approved by motivation theorists. It involves focusing on the task, rather than on the outcome. This gives pupils a sense of control over their own learning by encouraging them to break a task into manageable chunks – scaffolding in constructivist theory. It also removes the scope for damaging comparisons with other pupils which in Doyle's terms could lead to pupil unrest, in Seligman's terms (1975) to learned helplessness and in Covington's (1992) to self-worth motivation. The problem, of course, is that Doyle's solution faces precisely the same difficulties that we identified earlier. The structure of the school system in Britain is competitive, preoccupied with outcomes and normative comparisons. On the other hand, the counter to this objection is also the same, namely that some schools, and some teachers in every school, succeed in providing intellectually challenging teaching to which pupils of all abilities respond positively. They do not respond positively because they are told to try harder, as in some of the controlled attribution retraining experiments, but because they find most of the work interesting, because they know that their teacher expects them not to give up at the first sign of difficulty, because they know that their efforts will be valued, and because they have sufficient confidence in their teacher's judgement to believe they will be successful in the end.

From this analysis, achieving mastery orientation in pupils is as much an art as a set of skills. Rubin (1985) claimed that:

There is a striking quality to fine classrooms. Pupils are caught up in learning, excitement abounds; and playfulness and seriousness blend easily because the purposes are clear, the goals sensible and an unmistakable feeling of well-being prevails.

Artist teachers achieve these qualities by knowing both their subject matter and their students; by guiding the learning with deft control – a control that itself is born out of perception, intuition and creative impulse! (p. v)

Achieving mastery oriented pupils involves, by definition, them being interested in their own learning. An analogy with research on pupil behaviour is useful here. An enormous amount of work has been carried out on 'behaviour modification' techniques for reducing disruptive classroom behaviour (e.g. Wheldall *et al.*, 1983). Yet there is no evidence that teachers in schools in which pupil behaviour is hardly ever a problem have been trained in behaviour modification techniques. On the contrary, teachers only attend courses in these techniques when they find themselves working in schools where the problem is acute. Moreover, in spite of the fairly clear short-term success of these techniques, evidence of long-term change is conspicuously lacking. The solution to pupil behaviour problems does not lie in acquiring a set of behavioural techniques, even if many of these are used intuitively by teachers who do not have discipline problems. Similarly a considerable body of research has explored the possibility of changing motivational style, including Craske's (1988) study. These studies have provided valuable insights into motivational processes but they have the same limitation as behaviour management programmes. There is no panacea for developing mastery orientation and preventing maladaptive styles. We can, however, draw at least one conclusion from the evidence of school and teacher effectiveness in promoting pupils' learning, positive behaviour patterns and, implicitly, motivation. That is that they are all underpinned by a common set of values.

Conclusions: values as a neglected aspect of motivation research

Virtually every educational reform in the period 1979–1996 in Britain was opposed initially by teachers' professional associations. The government dutifully carried out a consultation process on each occasion, but subsequent changes to legislation placed before Parliament were never more than cosmetic. Galloway (1993) has argued that the legislation reflected a deep division within the ruling Conservative Party between those like Sir Keith Joseph who were motivated by a deep concern about the school system's contribution to the country's future economic competitiveness and those who were motivated by a deep mistrust of the egalitarianism implicit in raising standards among the under-achieving and mainly working-class pupils. This is the most logical explanation for one of the more bizarre contradictions in ministers' thinking; in spite of claiming that the National Curriculum aimed to raise standards, evidence that it was indeed achieving this aim, in the form of improved GCSE pass rates, was attributed both by the Prime Minister and by his Secretary of State to the examination boards lowering their standards. Teachers found themselves in a 'Catch 22': if examination results did not improve this would be evidence of their failure; when they did improve it was not evidence of their success.

In motivation theory, the effect of having one's advice systematically ignored and one's achievements systematically dismissed as misconceived should be to induce a feeling of learned helplessness. Nor is the consistent commitment to competitive market forces policies likely to encourage mastery or task orientation. By requiring schools to compete for pupils, and hence for funds, and by making schools more accountable to their local communities through publication of Ofsted reports and league tables of pupils' achievements, education policy has systematically encouraged ego orientation rather than mastery or task orientation, at least at the level of teacher motivation. Ego orientation, of course, is consistent with an objective of raising 'outcome' standards; the focus is on the end product, for example GCSE or A level passes rather than on the process of achieving these outcomes. The consequence of an ego oriented value position is that teachers of pupils who cannot compete successfully and teachers in schools at the foot of league tables become increasingly unlikely to feel that their efforts are worthwhile. This is seen in evidence that the gap between the most and least successful schools' pupils in Britain is wider than in many other countries (see Reynolds and Farrell, 1996). The result is likely to be that teachers adopt a work avoidance response in Nicholls' terms, arising from a feeling of helplessness, or a self-worth motivated response which uses rejection of government policies to legitimise reduction in commitment to high education standards.

Thankfully, government policy does not have much more power to influence the motivational styles which teachers and pupils adopt in school than it has to influence pupils' behaviour. In fact, its influence is minimal. The determining factors lie in the school and the classroom.

Moreover these factors are not a set of behaviour management techniques derived from learning theory but rather a commitment to a set of values based on mutual respect between pupils and teachers with an associated belief that if teachers set high standards pupils will achieve them.

It is this commitment to an agreed set of values which lies behind the complex but important notion of the hidden curriculum, defined by Galloway (1990) as:

The network of relationships in a school, between teachers, between pupils and between teachers and pupils which determine what teachers and pupils expect of themselves and of each other. (p. 15)

While this allows the possibility of school or classroom climate as a damaging influence, with low or negative expectations, it implicitly draws attention to its pervasiveness. It is this pervasiveness, or 'lived-in' culture which lies behind the school's influence on the motivational styles of its teachers and pupils. If teachers are to develop and maintain a mastery oriented approach they need recognition of their efforts from parents, governors and senior colleagues, support in helping them to overcome the difficulties inherent in any intellectually challenging teaching, and a sense that their own professional development is continuing – in other words that they are learning new things and mastering new skills.

For pupils the requirements are remarkably similar. They, too, need recognition of their efforts, and Rutter *et al.* (1979) found that rewards were widely distributed in the more effective schools, not confined to a small high-achieving minority. They also need realistic goals with an emphasis on strategies for achieving them. To support these goals they need a pastoral care system which serves to promote achievement rather than to act as an arm of the discipline system or as an explanation for low achievement (Williamson, 1980; Galloway, 1990).

These are needed by all pupils, but particularly by those we described at the start of this book as difficult to teach. Evidence from school effectiveness research suggests that these are the pupils whose long-term progress may be most affected, for better or worse, by factors in the school (Quinton and Rutter, 1988). School influences on the progress of high-achieving and intellectually more able pupils, and pupils with supportive families, tend to be less pronounced than on the progress and social behaviour of the more vulnerable pupils. These are pupils for whom realistic goals and adaptive motivational styles are most needed, for the rather obvious reason that they are least likely to be provided from sources outside the school.

Finally, while research on motivation of pupils and teachers in ordinary primary and secondary schools is still at an early stage, there are grounds for cautious optimism. School factors clearly exert an important influence. These include the structure of the tasks and the feedback which teachers provide. School factors are particularly important for pupils with low achievements but are by no means confined to these pupils. There are sound reasons for thinking that motivational style plays a central role in mediating different levels of school and teacher effectiveness. There is evidence from other research that schools have a particularly strong influence on the lives of those we have called difficult to teach. This influence is potentially beneficial but not necessarily so. The challenge of the next few years for research on motivation is to find ways to ensure that the influence is beneficial for more pupils in more schools. We have no expectation that all the arguments in this book will be accepted by academic colleagues or by teachers. We hope that they will nevertheless contribute to debate on ways to achieve this goal.

BIBLIOGRAPHY

Abramson, L.Y., Seligman, M.E.P. and Teasdale, J.D. (1978) Learned helplessness in humans: critique and reformulation. *Journal of Abnormal Psychology*, 87, 49–74.

Ainscow, M. and Florek, A. (eds) (1989) Special Educational Needs: Towards a Whole School Approach. London: David Fulton.

Alexander, R. (1992) *Policy and Practice in Primary Education*. London: Routledge.

Alexander, R., Rose, J. and Woodhead, C. (1992) *Curriculum Organisation and Classroom Practice in Primary Schools: A Discussion Paper*. London: DES.

Ames, C. (1984) Competitive, cooperative and individualistic goal structures: a cognitive-motivational analysis. In R.E. Ames and C. Ames (eds) *Research on Motivation in Education. Vol. 1: Student Motivation*. London: Academic Press.

Ames, C. (1987) The enhancement of student motivation. In M.L. Maehr and D.A. Kleiber (eds) *Advances in Motivation and Achievement. Vol. 5: Enhancing Motivation*. Greenwich, CT: JAI Press.

Ames, C. (1992) Classrooms: goals, structures and student motivation. *Journal of Educational Psychology*, 84, 261–71.

Ames, C. and Ames, R.E. (eds) (1989) *Research on Motivation in Education. Vol. 3: Goals and Cognitions*. London: Academic Press.

Ames, R.E. and Ames, C. (eds) (1984) *Research on Motivation in Education. Vol. 1: Student Motivation*. London: Academic Press.

Anderman, E.M. and Maehr, M.L. (1994) Motivation and schooling in the middle grades. *Review of Educational Research*, 64, 2, 287–309.

Andrews, G.R. and Debus, R.L. (1978) Persistence and the causal perception of failure: modifying cognitive attributions. *Journal of Educational Psychology,* 70, 154–66.

Atkinson, J. (1964) *An Introduction to Motivation*. Princeton, NJ: Van Nostrand.

Atkinson, J. and Raynor, J. (1974) *Motivation and Achievement*. Washington, DC: Winston.

Atkinson, J. and Raynor, J. (eds) (1978), *Personality, Motivation and Achievement*. Washington, DC: Hemisphere.

Ball, C. (1995) Presidential Address to the North of England Education Conference, England.

Bean, P. and Melville, J. (1989) *Children of the Lost Empire*. London: Unwin Hyman.

Bennett, N., Desforges, C., Cockburn, A. and Wilkinson, B. (1984) *The Quality of Pupil Learning Experiences*. London: Lawrence Erlbaum.

Blishen, E. (1955) *Roaring Boys*. London: Thames and Hudson.

Blumenfeld, P.C. (1992) Classroom learning and motivation: clarifying and expanding goal theory. *Journal of Educational Psychology*, 84, 272–81.

Blumenfeld, P.C., Hamilton, V.L., Bussert, S.T., Wessels, K. and Meece, J. (1983) Teacher talk and student thought: socialisation into the student role. In J.M. Levine and M.C. Wang (eds) *Teacher and Student Perceptions: Implications for Learning*. Hillsdale, NJ: Erlbaum.

Bowles, S. and Gintis, H. (1976) *Schooling in Capitalist America*. London: Routledge and Kegan Paul.

Brophy, J.E. (1985) Teacher-student interactions. In J.B. Dusek (ed.) *Teacher Expectancies*. Hillsdale, NJ: Erlbaum.

Brophy, J.E. and Evertson, C.M. (1978) Context variables in teaching. *Educational Psychologist*, 12, 310–16.

Burke, C. (1993) Transfer to secondary school: motivational consequences of transfer programmes. Unpublished dissertation for MA in Education, Lancaster University.

Burt (1974) *The Burt Word Reading Test (1974 Revision)*. Scottish Council for Research in Education Publication Number 66. London: Hodder & Stoughton.

Butler, R. (1994) Teacher communication and student interpretations: effects of teacher responses to failing students on attributional inferences in two age groups. *British Journal of Educational Psychology*, 64, 277–94.

Callaghan, J. (1976) Speech by the Prime Minister, the Rt. Hon. James Callaghan MP., at a foundation stone laying ceremony at Ruskin College, Oxford, 18 October (press release).

Cameron, J. and Pierce, W.D. (1994) Reinforcement, reward and intrinsic motivation: a meta-analysis. *Review of Educational Research*, 64, 363–423.

Chiland, C. and Young, J.G. (1990) *Why Children Reject School: View from Seven Countries*. London: Yale University Press.

Clark, C.M. and Peterson, P.L. (1986) Teachers' thought processes. In M. Wittrock (ed.) *Handbook of Research on Teaching*, 3rd Edition. New York: Macmillan.

Condry, J.D. and Chambers, J. (1978) Intrinsic motivation and the process of learning. In M.R. Lepper and D. Greene (eds), *The Hidden Costs of Reward: New Perspectives on the Psychology of Human Motivation*. Hillsdale, NJ: Erlbaum.

Connell, J.P. (1980) A multidimensional measure of children's perceptions of control. Unpublished manuscript, University of Denver.

Connell, J.P. and Tero, P.F. (1982) Aspects of continuity and change in children's self-regulated cognitions and affects within the academic domain. Unpublished manuscript, University of Rochester, New York.

Corrigan, P. (1979) *Schooling the Smash Street Kids*. London: Macmillan.

Covington, M.V. (1984) The motive for self-worth. In R.E. Ames and C. Ames (eds) *Research on Motivation in Education. Vol. 1: Student Motivation*. London: Academic Press.

Covington, M.V. (1992) *Making the Grade: A Self-worth Perspective on Motivation and School Reform*. Cambridge, MA: Cambridge University Press.

Cox, C.B. and Boyson, R. (1977) *Black Paper 1979*. London: Morris Temple Smith.

Craske, M.L. (1988) Learned helplessness, self-worth motivation and attribution retraining for primary school children. *British Journal of Educational Psychology*, 58, 152–64.

Csikszentmihalyi, M. (1992) *Flow: The Psychology of Happiness*. London: Rider.

Davies, L. (1982) *Pupil Power: Deviance and Gender in School*. Lewes: Falmer Press.

Davis, A. and Pettitt, D.J.M. (1995) Developing Understanding in Primary Mathematics. Lewes: Falmer.

De Charms, R. (1968) *Personal Causation*. New York: Academic Press.

De Charms, R. (1976) *Enhancing Motivation: Change in the Classroom*. New York: Irvington.

Dearing, R. (1994) *The National Curriculum and its Assessment. Final Report*. London: SCAA.

Deci, E.L. (1975) *Intrinsic Motivation*. New York: Plenum Press.

Deffenbacher, J.L. (1986) Cognitive and physiological components of test anxiety in real life exams. *Cognitive Therapy and Research*, 10, 635–44.

Delamont, S. and Galton, M. (1986) *Inside the Secondary Classroom*. London: Routledge and Kegan Paul.

Department of Education and Science (DES) (1978) *Special Educational Needs* (The Warnock Report). London: HMSO.

Doyle, W. (1983) Academic work. *Review of Educational Research*, 53, 159–99.

Doyle, W. (1986) Classroom organisation and management. In M.C. Wittrock (ed.) *Handbook of Research on Teaching*, 3rd Edition. New York: Macmillan.

Dweck, C.S. (1985) Intrinsic motivation, perceived control and self-evaluation maintenance: an achievement goal analysis. In C. Ames and R.E. Ames (eds) *Research on Motivation in Education. Vol. 2: The Classroom Milieu*. London: Academic Press.

Dweck, C.S. (1986) Motivational processes affecting learning. *American Psychologist*, 41, 1040–8.

Dweck, C.S. (1991) Self-theories and goals: their role in motivation, personality and development. *Nebraska Symposium on Motivation, Vol. 38*: University of Nebraska Press.

Dweck, C.S. and Bempechat, J. (1983) Children's theories of intelligence: consequences for learning. In S.G. Paris, G. Olsen and H. Stevenson (eds) *Learning and Motivation in the Classroom*. Hillsdale, NJ: Erlbaum.

Dweck, C.S. and Elliott, E.S. (1983) Achievement motivation. In P. Mussen (ed.) *Handbook of Child Psychology*. New York: Wiley.

Dweck, C.S. and Leggett, E.L. (1988) A social-cognitive approach to motivation and personality. *Psychological Review*, 95, 256–73.

Dweck, C.S. and Wortman, C.B. (1982) Learned helplessness, anxiety and achievement motivation. In H.W. Krohne and L. Laux (eds) *Achievement, Stress and Anxiety*. London: Hemisphere Publishing.

Dweck, C.S. (1975) The role of expectations and attributions in the alleviation of learned helplessness. *Journal of Personality and Social Psychology*, 31, 674–85.

Eccles, J. and Midgley, C. (1989) Stage-environment fit: developmentally appropriate classrooms for young adolescents. In C. Ames and R.E. Ames (eds) *Research on Motivation in Education. Vol. 3: Goals and Cognitions*. London: Academic Press.

Eccles, J. and Wigfield, A. (1985) Teacher expectations and student motivations. In J.B. Dursek (ed.) *Teacher Expectancies*. Hillsdale, NJ: Erlbaum.

Eccles, J., Midgley, C. and Adler, T. (1984) Grade-related changes in the school environment: effects on achievement motivation. In J.G. Nicholls (ed.) *Advances in Motivation and Achievement. Vol. 3: The Development of Achievement Motivation*. London: JAI Press.

Eccles, J., Wigfield, A. and Kaczala, C. (1988) Ontogeny of achievement related self and task beliefs. Unpublished manuscript, University of Michigan, Ann Arbor.

Elliott, E.S. and Dweck, C.S. (1988) Goals: an approach to motivation and achievement. *Journal of Personality and Social Psychology*, 54, 5–12.

Fogelman, K. (1976) *Britain's Sixteen Year Olds*. London: National Children's Bureau.

Frieze, I.H., Francis, W.D. and Hanusa, B.H. (1983) Defining success in classroom settings. In J. Levine and M. Wang (eds) *Teacher and Student Perceptions: Implications for Learning*. Hillsdale, NJ: Erlbaum.

Galloway, D. (1983) Disruptive pupils and effective pastoral care. *School Organisation*, 3, 245–54.

Galloway, D. (1985) *Schools, Pupils and Special Educational Needs.* London: Croom Helm.

Galloway, D. (1990) *Pupil Welfare and Counselling: An Approach to Personal and Social Education across the Curriculum.* London: Longman.

Galloway, D. (1993) Consensus, controversy and ambiguity in primary education. Inaugural Lecture of Professor of Primary Education, University of Durham School of Education.

Galloway, D. (1995)Truancy, delinquency and disruption: differential school influences. *Education Section Review (British Psychological Society),* 19, 2, 49–53.

Galloway, D. and Goodwin, C. (1987) *The Education of Disturbing Children: Pupils with Learning and Behaviour Difficulties.* London: Longman.

Galloway, D., Ball, T., Blomfield, D. and Seyd, R. (1982) *Schools and Disruptive Pupils.* London: Longman.

Galloway, D., Boswell, K., Panckhurst, F., Boswell, C. and Green, K. (1985) Sources of satisfaction and dissatisfaction for New Zealand primary school teachers. *Educational Research*, 27, 44–51.

Galloway, D., Armstrong, D. and Tomlinson, S. (1994) *The Assessment of Special Educational Needs: Whose Problem?* London: Longman.

Galloway, D., Leo, E., Rogers, C. and Armstrong, D. (1995) Motivational styles in English and mathematics among children identified as having special educational needs. *British Journal of Educational Psychology*, 65, 477–87.

Galloway, D., Leo, E., Rogers, C. and Armstrong, D. (1996) Maladaptive motivational style: the role of domain specific task demand in English and mathematics. *British Journal of Educational Psychology*, 66, 197–207.

Gotfried, E. (1981) Grade, sex and race differences in academic intrinsic motivation. Conference Paper, Annual Meeting of the American Educational Research Association, Los Angeles.

Hargreaves, D.H. (1967) *Social Relations in a Secondary School.* London: Routledge and Kegan Paul.

Hargreaves, D.H. (1982) *The Challenge for the Comprehensive School: Culture, Curriculum and Community.* London: Routledge and Kegan Paul.

Harris, A. (1995) *Effective Teaching. Research Matters, No.3.* London: School Improvement Network, Institute of Education.

Harter, S., Whitesell, N. and Kowalski, P. (1987) The effects of educational transitions on children's perceptions of competence and motivational orientation. Unpublished manuscript, University of Denver.

Her Majesty's Inspector of Schools (HMI) (1990) *Standards in Education, 1988–89*. London: DES.

Holdaway, E.A. (1978) Facet and overall satisfaction of teachers. *Education Administration Quarterly*, 14, 30–47.

Hull, C.L. (1943) *Principles of Behaviour*. New York: Appleton-Century-Crofts.

Hurt, J.S. (1988) *Outside the Mainstream*. London: Routledge and Kegan Paul.

Johnson, D.W. and Johnson, R.T. (1987) *Learning Together and Alone*, 2nd Edition. Englewood Cliffs, NJ: Prentice-Hall.

Jones, E.E., Kanouse, D.E., Kelley, H.H., Nisbett, R.E., Valins, S. and Weiner, B. (eds) (1972) *Attribution: Perceiving the Causes of Behaviour*. Morristown, NJ: General Learning Press.

Joseph, K. (1983) Address to Council of Local Education Authorities, 16 July. Unpublished.

Kelley, H.H. (1972) Causal schemata and the attribution process. In E.E. Jones, D.E. Kanouse, H.H. Kelley, R.E. Nisbett, S. Valins and B. Weiner (eds) *Attribution: Perceiving the Causes of Behaviour*. Morristown, NJ: General Learning Press.

Kelley, H.H. and Michela (1980) Attribution Theory and Research. In M.R. Rosenzweig and L.M. Parker (eds) *Annual Review of Psychology 31*, 457–501.

Kutnick, P. and Rogers, C.G. (1994) *Groups in Schools*. London: Cassell.

Kyriacou, C. (1991) *Essential Teaching Skills*. Oxford: Blackwell.

Lawrence, J. and Tucker, M. (1988) *Norwood was a Difficult School*. Basingstoke: Macmillan.

Leo, E.L. and Galloway, D. (1994) A questionnaire for identifying behavioural problems associated with maladaptive motivational style. *Educational and Child Psychology*, 11, 2, 91–9.

Little, A.W. (1985) The child's understanding of the causes of academic success and failure: a case study of British school-children. *British Journal of Educational Psychology*, 55, 11–23.

Livesley, W.J. and Bromley, D.B. (1973) *Person Perception in Childhood and Adolescence*. London: Wiley.

Macmillan (1985) *Macmillan Group Word Reading Test*. London: Macmillan Education.

Marsh, H.W. (1989) Age and sex effects in multiple dimensions of self-concept: preadolescence to early adulthood. *Journal of Educational Psychology*, 81, 417–30.

Marsh, H.W. (1990) A multidimensional, hierarchical model of self-concept: theoretical and empirical justification. *Educational Psychology Review*, 2, 77–172.

Marsh, H.W., Byrne, B.M. and Shavelson, R.J. (1988) A multifaceted academic self-concept: Its hierarchical structure and its relation to academic achievement. *Journal of Educational Psychology*, 80, 366–80.

Marsh, P., Rosser, E. and Harre, R. (1978) *The Rules of Disorder*. London: Routledge.

Marshall, H.H. (1992) Seeing, re-defining and supporting student learning. In H. Marshall (ed.) *Re-defining Student Learning: Roots of Educational Change*. Norwood, NJ: Ablex.

Mortimore, P., Sammons, P., Stoll, G., Lewis, D. and Ecob, R. (1988) *School Matters: The Junior Years*. Wells: Open Books.

National Curriculum Council (NCC) (1993) *The National Curriculum at Key Stages 1 and 2: Advice to the Secretary of State for Education*. York: NCC.

Nicholls, J.G. (1976) Effort is virtuous, but it's better to have ability: evaluative responses to perceptions of effort and ability. *Journal of Research in Personality*, 10, 306–15.

Nicholls, J.G. (1978) The development of the concepts of effort and ability, perception of academic attainment, and the understanding that difficult tasks require more ability. *Child Development*, 49, 800–14.

Nicholls, J.G. (1984) Achievement motivation: conceptions of ability, subjective experience, task choice and performance. *Psychological Review*, 91, 3, 328–46.

Nicholls, J.G. (1989) *The Competitive Ethos and Democratic Education*. Cambridge, MA: Harvard University Press.

Nicholls, J.G. and Miller, A.T. (1983) The differentiation of the concepts of difficulty and ability. *Child Development*, 54, 951–9.

Office for Standards in Education (Ofsted) (1993) *Curriculum Organisation and Classroom Practice in Primary Schools: A Follow-up Report*. London: Ofsted.

Pintrich, P.R., Marx, R.W. and Boyle, R.A. (1993) Beyond cold conceptual change: the role of motivational beliefs and classroom contextual factors in the process of conceptual change. *Review of Educational Research*, 63, 167–99.

Power, C. (1981) Changes in students' attitudes toward science in the transition between Australian elementary and secondary schools. *Journal of Research in Science Teaching*, 18, 33–9.

Prawat, R.S., Grissom, S. and Parish, T. (1979) Affective development in children, grades 3 through 12. *Journal of Genetic Psychology*, 135, 37–49.

Quinton, D. and Rutter, M. (1988) *Parenting Breakdown: The Making and Breaking of Inter-generational Links*. Aldershot: Avebury.

Rabinowitz, A. (1981) The range of solutions: a critical analysis. In B. Gillham (ed.) *Problem Behaviour in the Secondary School*. London: Croom Helm.

Ramasut, A. (1989) *Whole School Approaches to Special Needs: A Practical Guide for Secondary School Teachers*. Lewes: Falmer.

Reynolds, D. (1992) School effectiveness and school improvement: an updated review of the British literature. In D. Reynolds and P. Cuttance (eds) *School Effectiveness Research, Policy and Practice*. London: Cassell.

Reynolds, D. and Farrell, S. (1996) *Worlds Apart: A Review of International Surveys of Educational Achievement Involving England*. London: HMSO.

Reynolds, D. and Teddlie, C. (1996) *World Class Schools: A Preliminary Analysis of Data from the International School Effectiveness Research Project (ISERP)*. Newcastle: University of Newcastle Department of Education.

Rogers, C. and Kutnick, P. (1990) *The Social Psychology of the Primary School*. London: Routledge.

Rogers, C., Galloway, D., Armstrong, D., Jackson, C. and Leo, E.L. (1994) Changes in motivational style over the transfer from primary to secondary school: subject and dispositional effects. *Educational and Child Psychology*, 11, 26–38.

Rogers, C.G. (1978) The child's perception of other people. In H. McGurk (ed.) *Issues in Childhood Social Development*. London: Methuen.

Rogers, C.G. (1982) *A Social Psychology of Schooling*. London: Routledge and Kegan Paul.

Rubin, L. (1985) *Artistry and Teaching*. New York: Random House.

Rutter, M. (1976) Prospective studies to investigate behavioural change. In J.S. Strauss, H.M. Babigian and M. Roff (eds) *Methods of Longitudinal Research in Psychopathology*. New York: Plenum.

Rutter, M., Tizard, J. and Whitmore, K. (1970) *Education, Health and Behaviour*. London: Longman.

Rutter, M., Maughan, B., Mortimore, P. and Ouston, J. (1979) *Fifteen Thousand Hours: Secondary Schools and their Effects on Pupils*. London: Open Books.

Scottish Education Department (SED) (1978) *The Education of Pupils with Learning Difficulties in Primary and Secondary Schools: A Progress Report by Her Majesty's Inspectorate*. Edinburgh: HMSO.

Seligman, M.P. (1975) *Learned Helplessness: On Depression, Development and Death*. San Fransisco, CA: Freeman.

Shayer, M. and Adey, P.S. (1992) Accelerating the Development of Formal Thinking in Middle and High School Students, II: Post Project Effects on Science Achievement. *Journal of Research in Science Technology*, 29, 81–92.

Simmons, K. (1986) Painful extractions. *Times Educational Supplement*, 17 October.

Simmons, R.G., Rosenberg, F. and Rosenberg, M. (1973) Disturbance in the self-image at adolescence. *American Sociological Review*, 38, 553–68.

Slavin, R.E. (1983) *Cooperative Learning.* New York: Longman.

Slavin, R. (ed.) (1989) *School and Classroom Organisation.* London: Erlbaum.

Slavin, R. (1990) Cooperative learning. In C. Rogers and P. Kutnick (eds) *The Social Psychology of the Primary School.* London: Routledge.

Smith, D.J. and Tomlinson, S. (1989) *The School Effect: A Study of Multiracial Comprehensives.* London: Policy Studies Unit.

Spindler, G. (1987) *Education and Cultural Processes: Anthropological Approaches.* Prospect Heights: Waveland Press.

Stevenson, H. and Stigler, J. (1992) *The Learning Gap: Why are Schools Failing and what we can Learn from Japanese and Chinese Education?* New York: Simon and Schuster.

Thorndike, R.L., Hagen, E. and France, N. (1986) *Cognitive Ability Test.* Windsor: NFER. Nelson.

Tomlinson, S. (1982) *A Sociology of Special Education.* London: Routledge and Kegan Paul.

Warburton, S.J., Jenkins, W.L. and Coxhead, P. (1983) Science achievement and attitudes and the age of transfer to secondary school. *Educational Research*, 25, 177–83.

Weiner, B. (1974) Achievement motivation as conceptualized by an attribution theorist. In B. Weiner (ed.) *Achievement Motivation and Attribution Theory.* Morristown, NJ: General Learning Press.

Weiner, B. (1979) A theory of motivation for some classroom experiences. *Journal of Educational Psychology*, 71, 3–25.

Weiner, B. (1984) Principles for a theory of student motivation and their application within an attributional framework. In R.E. Ames and C. Ames (eds) *Research on Motivation in Education. Vol.1: Student Motivation.* London: Academy Press.

Weiner, B. (1986) *An Attributional Theory of Motivation and Emotion.* New York: Springer-Verlag.

Weiner, B. (1992) *Human Motivation: Metaphors, Theories and Research.* London: Sage.

Wheldall, K., Merrett, F.E. and Russell, A. (1983) *The Behavioural Approach to Teaching Package.* Birmingham: Centre of Child Study, University of Birmingham.

Wigfield, A. (1984) Relationships between ability perceptions, other achievement related beliefs and school performance. Conference Paper, Annual meeting of the Americal Educational Research Association, New Orleans.

Williamson, D. (1980) 'Pastoral care' or 'pastoralisation'? In R. Best, C. Jarvis and P. Ribbins (eds) *Perspectives on Pastoral Care.* London: Heinemann.

Willis, P. (1977) *Learning to Labour: How Working Class Kids get Working Class Jobs.* Farborough: Saxon House.

Youngman, M.B. (1978) Six reactions to school transfer. *British Journal of Educational Psychology*, 48, 280–9.

Yule, W. (1973) Differential prognosis of reading backwardness and specific reading retardation. *British Journal of Educational Psychology*, 43, 244–8.

Zebrowitz, L. (1990) *Social Perception*. Milton Keynes: Open University Press.

INDEX